NEW ENGLAND'S
Notable
WOMEN

NEW ENGLAND'S *Notable*

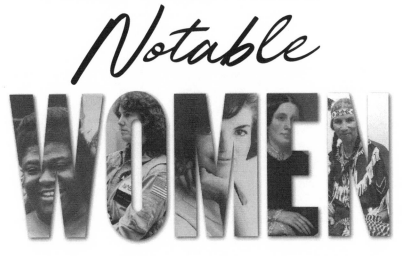

WOMEN

THE STORIES
AND SITES
OF TRAILBLAZERS
AND ACHIEVERS

PATRICIA HARRIS

Globe
Pequot

Essex, Connecticut

Globe
Pequot

An imprint of Globe Pequot, the trade division of The Rowman & Littlefield
Publishing Group, Inc.
4501 Forbes Blvd., Ste. 200
Lanham, MD 20706
www.rowman.com

Distributed by NATIONAL BOOK NETWORK

British Library Cataloguing in Publication Information available

Library of Congress Cataloging-in-Publication Data

Names: Harris, Patricia, 1949– author.
Title: New England's notable women : the stories and sites of trailblazers and achievers
/ Patricia Harris.
Description: Essex, Connecticut : Globe Pequot, [2023]
Identifiers: LCCN 2022008650 (print) | LCCN 2022008651 (ebook) | ISBN
9781493066018 (paper) | ISBN 9781493066025 (electronic)
Subjects: LCSH: Women—Homes and haunts—New England—Guidebooks. |
Historic sites—New England—Guidebooks. | Historic buildings—New England—
Guidebooks. | Women—New England—Biography. | New England—Guidebooks. |
New England—Biography.
Classification: LCC F5 .H378 2023 (print) | LCC F5 (ebook) | DDC 305.40974—
dc23/eng/20220321
LC record available at https://lccn.loc.gov/2022008650
LC ebook record available at https://lccn.loc.gov/2022008651

For all the women poised to do great things

CONTENTS

NEW HAMPSHIRE

VERMONT

MAINE

INTRODUCTION

I don't presume to compare myself to boomer generation punk seer Patti Smith. But as young girls, we were both captivated by Louisa May Alcott's novel *Little Women* and especially by Louisa's fictional counterpart, the spunky tomboy Jo March. Although I was the ultimate "Are we there yet?" kid, I persuaded my parents to drive me to Orchard House in Concord, Massachusetts. I was willing to endure the three-hour ride so that I could set foot in the home that Louisa shared with her parents and two sisters.

In the second-floor bedroom, I studied the little desk that her father had built between two windows. I imagined Louisa pulling up a chair, picking up a pen, and beginning to write "a girl's story." Now that I make my living as a writer, I am all the more amazed that she was able to complete *Little Women* in just three months, especially without a computer—or even a typewriter.

I don't know if it's the challenging weather, history of rebellion, or something else entirely, but New England has nurtured countless women who shook off traditional gender roles to forge their own destinies. They didn't set out to be role models, but that's what they became. Thanks to New England's preservationist bent, many places like Orchard House remain as touchstones to women's lives well lived.

I could fill volumes writing about New England women who have excelled in every field of human endeavor and have helped to make the world a better place. But for the purposes of this book, I have limited my scope to forty-five trailblazing women whom readers can meet not just on the page but also at sites that evoke their lives and achievements.

Just as we always seek to put a name with a face, we also form a deeper bond when we can picture a person in a particular place. That might be a museum, a family home, or a landscape. My many years writing about travel have shown me that places have the power to connect us to people we can't otherwise meet—and to open our minds to new possibilities.

For example, I hope that readers of this book will venture to the coast of Maine where Rachel Carson wrote books that launched the modern environmental movement. I've arranged this volume by state and grouped the sites geographically within each state. That way, readers can continue up the coast to share the iconic mountain view of Penobscot Bay that prompted Edna St. Vincent Millay to write the poem that launched her career.

As I worked on this book, I often thought about the message that these remarkable women would want to share. It boiled down to three simple, but power-ful, words: *Yes you can.*

I hope that this book finds its way into the hands of lots of young girls and encourages them to dream big. After all, Maya Lin was still an undergraduate stu-dent at Yale when she won the competition to create the Vietnam Veterans Memo-rial in Washington, DC. She is now one of the country's most accomplished and sought-after architects and sculptors.

The stories of New England women and their accomplishments provide lessons and inspiration for everyone. Maya Lin may have proved that you're never too young, but the example of Grandma Moses offers encouragement for the rest of us. She wasn't discovered as an artist until she was in her late seventies. You bet that you're never too old. And, of course, you can reinvent yourself at any age. Just look at the trajectory of Alva Smith Vanderbilt Belmont, a legendary hostess and socialite who presided over not one, but two grand Gilded Age mansions in Newport, Rhode Island. In middle age, she embraced the struggle for women's suffrage and turned her money and connections to powerful effect.

The women in this book often engaged in the struggle for human rights. In a perhaps apocryphal tale, Abraham Lincoln called Harriet Beecher Stowe "the little woman who wrote the book that started this great war." The author of *Uncle Tom's Cabin* spent her final years in Hartford, Connecticut, where her home is open to the public. A generation earlier, Prudence Crandall joined the struggle for equality in education when she admitted seventeen young women of African descent to her school for young women in Canterbury, Connecticut. Town leaders were so opposed that she was forced to close her school out of fear for her students' safety. Some things are worth doing even if you don't succeed. Crandall is now the Connecti-cut State Heroine and the names of the bigots who tormented her are historical footnotes.

Trust me, this book is not exclusively a journey through New England history—however fascinating it might be. Women writers and artists have opened our eyes to the limitless power of the human imagination. Follow the footsteps of poet Mary Oliver through the beech forest in Provincetown, Massachusetts. Or gaze at the powerful wooden constructions of Louise Nevelson, one of the most groundbreak-ing sculptors of the twentieth century. She grew up in Rockland, Maine, where the Farnsworth Art Museum owns one of the world's largest collections of her work. She was almost sixty years old before she finally received the art-world acclaim that she so richly deserved. Lesson? Never give up.

Women seem to have an instinct for starting museums. In Boston, Isabella Stew-art Gardner created such a "museum-worthy" collection that she built her own Ital-ian palace to display her art and artifacts. Princess Red Wing helped to establish the first and only museum of Indigenous peoples in Rhode Island. It will soon move into a much larger complex with more space to continue to tell the tales of New England's first inhabitants. In Vermont, Electra Havemeyer Webb was among the first to recognize the merit of American folk arts. Her Shelburne Museum brims with objects that capture the American spirit of ingenuity and that, in some cases, are just plain fun.

I felt privileged to literally follow in the footsteps of these utterly inspiring women. I imagined breathing in their spirit in every step. Each one of them is proof that nothing is beyond our grasp. *Yes you can.*

Born on tiny Nantucket island, Maria Mitchell literally reached for the stars. Along the way she compiled an amazing number of "firsts." To name a few, she was the first American to discover a comet, the first woman allowed into the Vatican observatory, and the first woman elected to the American Academy of Arts and Sciences. When she accepted a position at newly founded Vassar College, she became the first female astronomy professor in the United States.

Mitchell must have left shards of glass in her wake. Once you've broken one glass ceiling—go ahead and break another.

Patricia Harris
Cambridge, Massachusetts

CONNECTICUT

MABEL OSGOOD WRIGHT'S BIRD SANCTUARY

Birdcraft Museum and Sanctuary, 314 Unquowa Road, Fairfield; 203-259-0416; ctaudubon.org/birdcraft-home; sanctuary open year-round; free

Library of Congress

You might say that medicine's loss was the environment's gain. Thwarted in her goal to become a physician, Mabel Osgood Wright instead became a leader in the nascent conservation movement at the turn of the twentieth century.

Mabel was the youngest of three daughters of prominent Unitarian minister Samuel Osgood and his wife, Ellen. She was born in New York City on January 26, 1859, into a family that prized education. Mabel attended private schools and met the writers, artists, and intellectuals who were part of her father's circle. But Samuel Osgood's enlightened attitude extended only so far. Declaring that medicine was not a proper profession for women, he refused his daughter's request to attend Cornell Medical School.

The family summered at Mosswood, their eighteen-room country home on eight acres in Fairfield. It was here that Mabel discovered her life's work by yoking her interest in science to her love of nature. Eager to share her observations of the natural world with city dwellers, she published her first nature essay in the *New York Evening Post* when she was sixteen years old.

In 1884, Mabel married James Osborne Wright, a British dealer in art and rare books who shared her interests in gardening and the outdoors. After a stay in Europe, the couple returned to the United States and divided their time between Mosswood and New York City.

A decade after her marriage, Mabel Osgood Wright published *The Friendship of Nature: A New England Chronicle of Birds and Flowers*, illustrating her collection of nature essays with her own photographs. Fairfield resident and Macmillan publisher George Brett then encouraged her to write a guide to birds. Bird-watching had emerged as a popular pastime for those with the leisure to pursue it, but few books were targeted to general audiences.

Wright embarked on the project with the aim of writing "a popular field book to New England birds, upon a plan that will render the subject interesting and lucid." She spent two winters conducting research in the ornithology department of the American Museum of Natural History under the tutelage of curator Joel Allen and assistant curator Frank Chapman.

Birdcraft: A Field Book of Two Hundred Song, Game, and Water Birds was published in 1895. It became the prototype of the modern bird field guide for a popular audience, thanks to striking illustrations by John James Audubon and Louis Agassiz Fuertes and Wright's detailed descriptions of habitat, song, appearance, and behavior of each bird. An immediate success, the book was reprinted nine times. A couple of years later, Wright collaborated with ornithologist Elliott Coues to publish *Citizen Bird: Scenes from Bird-Life in Plain English for Beginners*, an early and influential guide to the practice of birding. To cultivate the next generation of environmentalists, she also wrote several books for children and often visited schools to share her knowledge of birds.

Wright hardly stopped there. In 1898, she founded the Connecticut Audubon Society to fill the gap left when the original national Audubon folded after a decade in 1896. The Connecticut Audubon Society was one of the earliest state organizations. The Massachusetts Audubon Society (now Mass Audubon) was the first, founded in 1896 by Minna B. Hall and Harriet Lawrence Hemenway. Women, in fact, played major roles in founding state Audubon societies and in other early conservation efforts.

Wright was the first president of the Connecticut Audubon Society and set the organization on the two-pronged course of promoting conservation through both education and legislation. Books such as hers encouraged a greater appreciation of the delicate balance of the human and natural worlds. But more definitive action was often necessary. Connecticut Audubon lobbied for legislation to protect sandpipers, to protect birds and their eggs from collectors, and to eliminate a bounty on bald eagles. The organization also backed the creation of national parks and forests.

An issue of paramount importance to the Audubon societies was the so-called plume trade. To satisfy women's desire for fashionable hats, market hunters slaughtered thousands of birds each year for their feathers, often leaving defenseless hatchlings in their nests. This practice was finally banned with the passage of the Weeks-McLean Migratory Bird Act in 1913, still cited as a pivotal piece of legislation in the American conservation movement.

Wright's most lasting legacy is Birdcraft Sanctuary, the first private songbird refuge in the country. She created it on ten acres of land donated to the Connecticut Audubon Society by her friend Annie Burr Jennings, a Standard Oil heiress and philanthropist. The women selected a plot of land near the Fairfield train station. The choice was deliberate. Wright wrote that introducing "people to the bird in the

bush is the way to create a public sentiment to keep it there." Proximity to public transportation, she reasoned, would make it easy to visit the sanctuary. Whether by plan or luck, the site also proved to be the first welcoming patch of green for exhausted migrating birds crossing Long Island Sound heading north from the New Jersey shore.

Wright laid out the guidelines for the construction of the sanctuary, including a cat-proof fence encircling the entire property. She specified that it should have a pond dug that would be fed by existing springs and called for planting bird-friendly shrubs. She drew trails so that humans could observe the birds without disturbing them and added seats, observation shelters, and birdbaths to the landscape. The society also constructed a caretaker's cottage, which served as its headquarters. Birdcraft, named for Wright's famous book, opened in October 1914. Public interest was immediate and intense, and Birdcraft remains especially popular during spring and fall songbird migrations.

Wright's former teacher Frank Chapman wrote of Birdcraft in *Bird-Lore*, the precursor to *Audubon* magazine. He noted that "ten acres cannot harbor many birds ... but the idea which they embody can reach to the ends of the earth."

Mabel Osgood Wright died on July 16, 1934, so she did not have to endure the construction of Interstate 95 in the 1950s that destroyed nearly half of her beloved Birdcraft. But good ideas have a way of persevering. Today's six-acre sanctuary, sandwiched between a busy highway and a railroad line, remains a welcoming oasis for more than 135 bird species and for those whose hearts soar when they see and hear them. Dozens of resident species nest within the sanctuary. Moreover, birders who flock to Birdcraft report as many as twenty species of colorful warblers making spring migration rest stops on any given day.

KATHLEEN MOORE'S LIGHTHOUSE POST
Black Rock Harbor Lighthouse on Fayerweather Island; access from Seaside Park, 1 Barnum Dyke, Bridgeport; 203-576-7233; bridgeportct.gov; park open year-round; admission charged

Career paths were pretty limited for women in the nineteenth century. According to the United States Coast Guard, for example, a position as a lighthouse keeper was one of the few options available for women seeking a non-clerical job with the government. That's quite a leap, from filing and writing documents by hand to tending a light and rescuing mariners at sea. Perhaps no woman knew both the perils and the daily routine of the job better than Kathleen Moore. She served as keeper of the Black Rock Harbor Lighthouse on Fayerweather Island from 1817 to 1878.

The Historian's Office of the United States Coast Guard has compiled a list of 175 women who have worked as lighthouse keepers or in related administrative roles. That record shows that Moore was only the second woman to hold the position of lighthouse keeper. (The first was Hannah Thomas, who served at Gurnet Point in Massachusetts from 1776 to 1786.) Kathleen Moore may not have been the first, but she holds the record as the longest-serving female lighthouse keeper—with a remarkable sixty-one years of service.

Moore's date of birth seems lost to history, although it may be as late as 1812. According to Coast Guard records, she began to assume some light-keeper duties around 1817, less than a decade after the light station was established on Fayerweather Island. Many women stepped into the role of lighthouse keeper when their husbands became ill or died. In a slight twist, Kathleen filled in for her father, Stephen Moore. Injuries made it increasingly

difficult for him to handle the job, especially carrying oil up the narrow steps to the lantern room where eight oil lamps with fourteen-inch reflectors sent a beam of light out into the night sky. Chalk it up, perhaps, to government bureaucracy, but Kathleen Moore had to wait until after her father's death in 1871 to be officially recognized as the head lighthouse keeper.

But she didn't need a title to do her job of guiding ships through the busy channels of Long Island Sound. She took that duty seriously. In the 1854 edition of *Noble Deeds of American Women*, Moore was lauded as "ever ready to lend a helping hand, and shrinks from no danger, if duty points the way." Adept at handling boats, Moore was credited with saving the lives of twenty-one mariners. She nursed some of them back to health on the island and always regretted the ones she was unable to bring safely to shore.

When she was interviewed late in her life, Moore enjoyed looking back on the challenges and satisfactions of her lighthouse years. "Sometimes there were more than two hundred sailing vessels in here at night," she recalled, "and some nights there were as many as three or four wrecks." Keeping the beam lit during gusty winds was always a trial. Moore spent many sleepless nights watching over the lanterns.

The storms punctuated an otherwise routine, if demanding, way of life. Moore often rowed the Black Rock entrance channel to Bridgeport when the weather allowed, but, by necessity, she was as self-sufficient as possible. She planted and tended a garden and spent considerable time collecting rainwater, which was the island's only source of freshwater. She cultivated oyster beds in Long Island Sound, gathering and seeding her own spat. She also cared for her Newfoundland dogs and carved duck decoys to sell to hunters and tourists.

Her parents lived on the island for many years, and Moore claimed never to be bothered by the isolation of island life. "I never had time to get lonely," she told an interviewer. "I had a lot of poultry and two cows to care for, and each year raised twenty sheep, doing the shearing myself—and the killing when necessary."

Moore described the sea as a "treacherous friend," but one that she came to know well. "You see," she told a reporter, "I had done all this for so many years, and I knew no other life, so I was sort of fitted for it."

When Moore finally retired in 1878 she moved ashore and bought a house near the harbor in the Black Rock neighborhood of Bridgeport. She lived there until her death in 1899. But she has not been forgotten. In 2014, the United States Coast Guard cutter *Kathleen Moore* was commissioned in her honor. At the time, Captain Ed Cubanski, the Coast Guard's Commander of Long Island Sound, noted that Moore "was a life saver in the 1800s yet she wasn't allowed to vote."

Black Rock Harbor Light was deactivated in 1932. The forty-foot-tall octagonal tower, which dates from 1823, was restored in 1980. It is not open to the public but can be reached by walking along the 3,000-foot-long stone breakwater that now connects Fayerweather Island to the western end of Bridgeport's Seaside Park. The 325-acre park stretches nearly three miles along Long Island Sound and was one of the first marine rural parks in the country.

MAYA LIN'S LAUNCHING PAD
Yale University, Mead Visitor Center, 149 Elm Street, New Haven; 203-432-2300; visitorcenter.yale.edu; open year-round; free

Sharon Styer

Maya Lin only spent a few years at Yale University, but she used her time well. As a twenty-one-year-old senior, Lin famously submitted a design for the Vietnam Veterans Memorial to be built on the National Mall in Washington, DC. She received a grade of B for the class project, but the jury of architects and sculptors was more enthusiastic. They unanimously selected Lin's design from more than 1,400 anonymous entries.

The jurors recognized the power of Lin's proposal for two walls of black granite grounded in the earth and carrying the names of more than 58,000 dead and missing. During her first two years at Yale, Lin had watched as stonecutters etched the names of the university's casualties of the Vietnam War onto the Memorial Rotunda in Woolsey Hall. "I had never been able to resist touching the names cut into these marble walls," Lin later recalled. "I think it made a lasting impression on me, the sense of the power of a name."

Controversial at first for its departure from traditional figurative memorial sculpture, the Vietnam Veterans Memorial has become what architecture critic Paul Goldberger has called "as moving and awesome and popular a piece of memorial architecture as exists anywhere in the world." Marching across the wall in chronological order, the names achieve a quiet majesty.

Lin received her bachelor of arts degree from Yale in 1981 and attended the dedication ceremony for the Vietnam Veterans Memorial in November of the following year. She returned to Yale to earn a master of architecture degree in 1986. She was well on her way to establishing herself as one of the country's most thoughtful and respected public artists. And she was not yet thirty years old.

Lin was born on October 5, 1959, in Athens, Ohio, and grew up in a household that prized creativity. Her parents, both immigrants from China, were professors at Ohio University. Her father, Henry Huan Lin, a ceramist, established the university's ceramics program and became dean of the College of Fine Arts. Her mother, Julia Chang Lin, a poet, taught literature and translated the works of contemporary Chinese poets.

In her 2000 book *Boundaries*, Lin notes, "My work originates from a simple desire to make people aware of their surroundings." Currently based in a studio in New York, she has built an impressive portfolio of work that spans art, architecture, and landscape. For the 1989 Civil Rights Memorial in Montgomery, Alabama, Lin transformed water from a decorative sculptural feature into an emotional force that captures the power of Martin Luther King, Jr.'s "I Have a Dream" speech. The design incorporates a curved wall of water and a circular stone water table. Inscriptions on the water table trace the major events of the struggle for equal rights from 1954 to 1968 and honor those whose lives were lost.

Lin's notable projects are too numerous to list. Over several years, for example, she reshaped a farm in Clinton, Tennessee, that had belonged to writer Alex Haley. She reconceived an old barn as the 1999 Langston Hughes Library and designed the 2004 Riggio-Lynch Interfaith Chapel. In 2009, Lin completed her largest site-specific installation at Storm King Art Center in New Windsor, New York. Called *Storm King Wavefield*, it features four acres of undulating waves of grass-covered earth that range from ten to fifteen feet high, trough to crest. Simple yet profound, the wavefield evokes an oceanic sensation by making solid ground mimic the fluidity of the sea.

David Lyon

When Yale University decided to commission a work of sculpture to mark the twentieth anniversary of admitting women as undergraduate students, there was truly only one logical choice. Completed in 1993, *The Women's Table*, located on Rose Walk in front of the Sterling Memorial Library, features an ellipse of blue stone inscribed with a spiral that enumerates the gradually swelling presence of women at the once all-male university. The tight spiral begins with a march of zeros until it finally records thirteen women enrolled in the School of Fine Arts in 1873. In 1969, the year that Yale became coed, the number of women climbed to 1,718. From then on, the spiral marks steady progress to 4,273 women when Lin graduated in 1981, and 5,225 women in 1993. Water bubbles from the center and washes across the surface and over the edge. The spiral itself opens infinitely wider as women gain a greater foothold in the university.

As Lin has noted, "The choice of a spiral was made to indicate a beginning but to leave the future open." In many ways, that spiral is a good metaphor for Lin's own experience at Yale.

Lin Makes Her Mark in New England

Maya Lin has graced New England with several other sculptural and architectural projects. For *The Meeting Room*, completed in 2013 on Queen Anne Square in Newport, Rhode Island, she created stone foundations that recall three centuries of buildings that had stood on the site. Supported by the Newport Restoration Foundation (see page 47), the spaces have become popular for private contemplation and small gatherings. In 2015, she completed *Under the Laurentide* for the Brown University campus in Providence, Rhode Island. She carved the spiderweb of waterways in and surrounding Narragansett Bay on a round of granite that reveals the terrain normally hidden by the sea.

That same year, Lin created the master plan for an expansion of the campus of Novartis Institutes for BioMedical Research on Massachusetts Avenue in Cambridge, Massachusetts. A small garden within the three-building complex is open to the public. As part of the project, she designed the 181 Massachusetts Avenue building. The lacy, pierced stone facade has made the building a new city landmark. For Smith College (her mother's alma mater) in Northampton, Massachusetts, Lin remodeled and expanded the 1909 Neilson Library using the principles of sustainable design. Completed in 2021, it is the first college library in her portfolio. The transformation created a light-filled complex lit during the day by a central oculus. Lin's accompanying landscaping plan of walks and plantings restores a flow of pedestrian traffic through the campus.

CAROLINE FERRIDAY'S COUNTRY HOME
Bellamy-Ferriday House & Garden, 9 North Main Street, Bethlehem;
203-266-7596; ctlandmarks.org; open May through October;
admission charged

Visitors to this eighteenth-century house are rarely surprised that Caroline Ferriday, its last owner, filled it with furnishings and antiques that reflected her interest in history and her penchant for the Colonial Revival style that held sway in the early decades of the twentieth century. It's more intriguing to discover the carefully framed certificate that recognizes her as a recipient of the French Legion of Honor. The house, in fact, relates the story of a woman who was both an antiquarian and a determined humanitarian.

Caroline Ferriday's interest in colonial history was sparked by her curiosity about the home's first owner, the Reverend Joseph Bellamy (1719–1790), an evangelical preacher and disciple of fire-and-brimstone preacher Jonathan Edwards. Bellamy originally built a modest four-room house when he was called to the Congregational church in Bethlehem in the early 1750s. In the next decade, he enlarged the home as he grew in stature as a well-known preacher and author.

The home remained in the Bellamy family until 1868, when it passed to a succession of unrelated owners. Its modern chapter began in 1912 when Henry McKeen Ferriday, a wealthy New York dry goods merchant, purchased the property for a

David Lyon

David Lyon

summer estate. He and his wife, Eliza Mitchell Ferriday, had one child, Caroline, who was born on July 3, 1902. In addition to introducing his daughter to the Connecticut countryside, Henry Ferriday also passed on his passion for French life and culture. Both would shape the course of Caroline's life.

Henry Ferriday died in 1914 and did not live to see the rundown home transformed into a fine country house with modern heat, electricity, and plumbing. Mother and daughter also created a showcase formal garden inspired (so the story goes) by the medallion on a Persian carpet. The garden is at its best in early summer when the roses and peonies are in bloom. Caroline, who was especially devoted to rose propagation and cultivation, continued to spend summers here for the rest of her life.

Tours of the house begin in the formal dining room, where the low ceilings identify it as part of Bellamy's original small house. The beginning of a later addition is marked by the high ceilings of the adjoining sitting room, Caroline's favorite spot in the house. She would sit in a pink armchair by the window to enjoy tea in the morning and return for gin martinis in the afternoon. A narrow passage leads to the library, where the walls almost groan with the thousand books in Caroline's library. Reflecting her interests in gardening, drama, poetry, and history, the library places special emphasis on Joseph Bellamy, early New England life, and World War II. Photos arrayed on a chaise longue depict Caroline in several of her roles as an actress.

She pursued an acting career in the 1920s and early 1930s, but eventually abandoned it for more humanitarian pursuits. As Europe moved ever closer to war in the late 1930s, she turned her attention to aiding refugees as a volunteer at the French consulate in New York. She was also quick to join France Forever, the Fighting French Committee in America, formed to support the Free French movement led in exile by General Charles de Gaulle.

Several years later, Ferriday became involved with ADIR, the National Association of Deportees and Internees of the Resistance. The organization was founded in 1945 by French women of the resistance movement who had been interned in German camps. A number of political prisoners, including Genevieve de Gaulle, niece of Charles de Gaulle, were interned at Ravensbrück, a forced labor camp for women located about fifty miles north of Berlin. All the women faced harsh working conditions and threat of execution. In addition, seventy-four women, primarily from Poland, were subjected to cruel medical experiments to test the efficacy of sulfa drugs to fight infection.

Liberated by the Russians, Ravensbrück was not as widely known in the United States as such notorious camps as Auschwitz-Birkenau, the largest of the Nazi extermination camps. Ferriday learned about Ravensbrück through ADIR and launched a campaign to help the women who had survived the medical experimentation. With the assistance of *Saturday Review* editor Norman Cousins, she visited Warsaw several times, negotiated with Polish officials, and met and gained the trust of the Polish women who were still suffering the effects of the horrors inflicted on them. Writing of the experience in the *Saturday Review*, Cousins noted that "Caroline Ferriday has an almost magical gift for inspiring confidence."

Thirty-five of the surviving women spent a year—from December 1958 to December 1959—in the United States to receive medical treatment. They also met with members of Congress in Washington, DC, and embarked on a cross-country tour to bring the atrocities at Ravensbrück to light. With pressure from Ferriday and others, the German government eventually agreed to make reparations to the survivors. A small group spent Christmas with Ferriday at her Bethlehem home, and she remained in contact with several of the women after they returned to Europe.

Ferriday threw herself into other causes, including the American civil rights movement. She also helped to establish the first Black bank in Harlem. But her deeply personal commitment to the Ravensbrück women may have been the defining moment in a life that came to focus on helping others. It did not go unrecognized. The certificate of the French Legion of Honor is displayed in the parlor of Ferriday's Bethlehem home. Established by Napoleon Bonaparte in 1802, it is the country's highest order of merit. Next to it is a smaller certificate for the Cross of Lorraine, the symbol that Charles de Gaulle chose for the Free French forces in World War II.

Many of the tributes to Caroline Ferriday were more personal. Following her death on April 27, 1990, Genevieve de Gaulle expressed the opinion of many women when she wrote that Ferriday was "a sister to everyone."

THEODATE POPE RIDDLE'S FAMILY HOME
Hill-Stead Museum, 35 Mountain Road, Farmington; 860-677-4787; hillstead.org; open year-round; admission charged

Few properties receive the designation of National Historic Landmark even once. Hill-Stead, on the other hand, has been so honored twice. The Pope family home was first recognized in 1991. Three decades later, the US Secretary of the Interior went a step further by conferring the distinction on the entire 152-acre estate, its structures, and its landscape design. That's not bad for the first major project of largely self-taught architect Theodate Pope Riddle.

Bachrach Studios, Archives, Hill-Stead Museum, Farmington, CT

Theodate Pope was born on February 2, 1867, and grew up in Cleveland, Ohio, as the only child of industrialist Alfred Pope and Ada Brooks Pope. From 1886 to 1888 she studied at Miss Porter's School in Farmington, Connecticut, then a finishing school where young ladies of means would polish their social graces. Theodate also came to appreciate the landscape of central Connecticut and the character and integrity of the region's historic homes.

Soon after she left Miss Porter's, Theodate joined her parents on an extended grand tour of Europe. As she traveled, she pondered her future. Young women of her social class were not expected to pursue careers, but Theodate thought of becoming an artist or a writer. Perhaps due to her habit of sketching buildings, her father suggested architecture. It was a bold choice, given that the field was dominated by men. Louise Blanchard Bethune, the first American woman to work as a professional architect, had opened her office only a few years earlier, in 1881.

In her diary entry of January 26, 1889, Theodate wrote, "I am quite interested in Papa's sugestion [*sic*] of my studying architecture." Later, on February 13, she noted, "My interest in architecture has lasted perhaps two weeks (may it last much longer). I mean to read up on the subject."

For his part, Alfred Pope began to build a major collection of Impressionist paintings by purchasing seminal works by Claude Monet and Edgar Degas. Over time, he added pieces by Mary Cassatt, Édouard Manet, Pierre-Auguste Renoir, Camille Pissarro, and James McNeill Whistler.

When the family returned to the United States in 1890, Theodate settled in Farmington and pursued architecture with a greater sense of purpose than her journal writings might have suggested. She began to assemble an architecture library and arranged for private tutorials from Princeton University professors. She also gained practical experience by living in and restoring an eighteenth-century saltbox house.

It was just a warm-up for her next project: a 33,000-square-foot country home on 250 acres. Alfred Pope purchased the land in 1898 and put the design of the house and gardens in his daughter's hands. At her father's urging, Theodate consulted with the esteemed architectural firm of McKim, Mead & White, but she dictated the terms of the relationship. In a letter to the architects, she wrote that "as it is my plan, I expect to decide on all the details as well as all the more important questions of plan that may arise. That must be clearly understood at the outset, so as to save unnecessary friction in the future. In other words, it will be a Pope house instead of a McKim, Mead, and White."

Work began in 1899 and was completed by June 1901. The Colonial Revival home with its references to traditional farmhouse style garnered almost immediate

David Lyon

David Lyon

attention in the magazines of the day. It was featured in the November 1902 *Architectural Review* and then again in the August 1906 *Architectural Record*.

Even in such a large home, Theodate created a sense of domestic ease. The Popes entertained often and enjoyed welcoming guests to the drawing room, where Alfred hung his Monet haystacks and Degas portraits. The elder Popes—and later Theodate and her diplomat husband—often hosted dinner parties in the large dining room off the coach entrance. Theodate's personality emerges in the library. The book collection includes works on the supernatural (she was obsessed with contacting her father after his death in 1913) and volumes by such house guests as William and Henry James.

Theodate most likely met pioneer landscape designer Beatrix Farrand (see page 179) through their mutual friend, novelist Henry James. She engaged Farrand to create the lovely Sunken Garden across the driveway from the front entrance of the house. Hill-Stead Museum has restored the garden using Farrand's 1920 planting plan. The design illustrates her deft touch at mixing plants to ensure a succession of color and scent.

By the time Theodate was licensed as an architect in New York in 1916, she had already designed several private homes as well as the Westover School for Girls in Middlebury and Hop Brook School in Naugatuck. In the early 1920s, she was commissioned to reconstruct Theodore Roosevelt's birthplace in New York City. She also founded Avon Old Farms, a private school for boys, and designed a village-like campus inspired by the architecture of the English Cotswolds. It opened in 1927 as a memorial to her father. She was finally licensed as the sixth woman architect in Connecticut in 1933—the first year that the state gave licenses to women.

In addition to her architecture practice, Theodate found time for other pursuits. She supported the women's suffrage movement and hosted British suffragist Emmeline Pankhurst for lunch at Hill-Stead before Pankhurst delivered her famous "Freedom or Death" speech in Hartford. Theodate was one of the survivors of the torpedoing and sinking of the British cruise ship RMS *Lusitania* in 1915. The next year, at age forty-nine, she married former American diplomat John Wallace Riddle. The couple spent much of their time at Hill-Stead, but also traveled extensively in Europe, Egypt, China, Japan, and Korea.

Upon her death on August 30, 1946, Theodate left a fifty-page document making Hill-Stead into a museum and dictating how it was to be displayed and where every work of art was to be hung. Hill-Stead opened to the public the following year. It remains a model of an early twentieth-century country estate and a monument to the taste and talent of Theodate Pope Riddle.

Writing of her in 2010, architectural historian James O'Gorman noted, "Many an architect has had to wait for years of experience to accomplish work of the personality, quality, and importance that she saw rise from her ideas on the knoll at Farmington."

FLORENCE GRISWOLD'S ART COLONY BOARDINGHOUSE

Florence Griswold Museum, 96 Lyme Street, Old Lyme; 860-434-5542; florencegriswoldmuseum.org; open year-round; admission charged

Florence Griswold was born on December 25, 1850, in one of the finest mansions in the seafaring town of Old Lyme. Her father, Robert Griswold, bought the property about a decade earlier when he and Helen Powers married. The late Georgian–style building with tall white columns was a fitting home for a man of his standing in the community. After all, the sea captain could trace his roots back to the town's early seventeenth-century founders and to two Connecticut governors.

Florence was a child when the family's fortunes began to decline, but she and her two sisters still received the finishing school education enjoyed by young women of their social class. Studies in music, painting, foreign languages, and needle arts were intended to bring them success as gracious and cultured wives. Florence instead channeled her talents—she was fluent in French and played the guitar, harp, and piano—into nurturing one of the country's most famous early twentieth-century art colonies.

Simply put, she was the right woman in the right place at the right time. As the new century began, Florence was the last member of the family left in the big

David Lyon

David Lyon

but rundown home. To keep herself afloat, she sold flowers and vegetables from her gardens and took in a few seasonal boarders who sought to escape Boston and New York for a rustic idyll on the Connecticut coast.

Prominent landscape painter and art teacher Henry Ward Ranger discovered Old Lyme in 1899. He was in quest for a spot where he could create an American art colony akin to Barbizon or Giverny in France—a place where artists could find inspiration in the landscape and a sense of camaraderie in their shared purpose. In terms of scenery, Old Lyme had it all: saltwater marshes, a sheltered shoreline, open meadows, quiet rivers, farms, and dignified historic buildings. The town also had Florence Griswold, with her gracious old house and welcoming personality.

Ranger boarded at the Griswold house during his first foray to Old Lyme, and over the winter he recruited fellow New York painters to join him on the Connecticut coast. He promised a landscape "waiting to be painted" and a congenial landlady with a mansion set on eleven acres along the banks of the Lieutenant River.

Griswold embraced her role as what the *Hartford Courant* would describe a century later as "venerated earth mother" of a bohemian group of artists. She created more bedrooms in her attic and turned outbuildings into studios. Miss Florence, as she was called, organized picnics, canoe trips, and wagon rides as well as evening theatrical performances. Sometimes she would entertain the artists by playing her harp. She hired a cook to provide three meals a day; a horn summoned the artists from their easels to lunch.

Miss Florence was also determined to help her "boys," as she affectionately called them, achieve artistic success. She found lost brushes, shipped canvases, and drew on her own cultivated taste to offer encouragement. Ever practical, she set up a gallery in her front hall to sell the artists' work. She joined some of the Old Lyme artists in launching annual summer art exhibits and establishing the first artist-financed cooperative gallery in the country. Both are now staples of the art colony experience.

Over the years, about 200 artists boarded at the Griswold house. Most were, in fact, men, although a few women joined the group and wives occasionally accompanied their artist husbands. The artists were rarely neophytes. Most had established careers or were about to make their breakthrough. Impressionist painters Childe Hassam and Willard Metcalf were perhaps the best known. As the artists' reputations grew, so did the stature of Old Lyme. By 1907, a newspaper article noted that "with no less enthusiasm than the gold hunters of '49, the picture makers have chosen Lyme as the place to swarm."

For the first two decades of the twentieth century, the little town hosted one of the country's most celebrated art colonies. At its center were Miss Florence and her boardinghouse. Artists who made the pilgrimage to Old Lyme—but had to seek other lodgings—called Miss Florence's home the "Holy House."

David Lyon

David Lyon

The first floor replicates the look of 1910, when the art colony was at its peak. Paintings, including a portrait of Miss Florence, hang in the makeshift gallery in the broad center hall. Two bedrooms are off the hall. Miss Florence's private retreat features floral wallpaper and a patchwork quilt on the bed. The front of the house is dominated by the parlor, where artists would gather in the evening for card games, discussions, or other entertainment. A harp sits in one corner.

It's easiest to imagine Miss Florence presiding over her "boys" in the dining room. After the artist boarders had painted scenes on most of the doors on the first floor, mahogany panels were set in the dining room walls so that the exuberant exercise could continue. A committee of artists would choose who would paint a panel, a sure sign of status in Old Lyme. The forty-one panels chronicle the changing styles in American painting in the early twentieth century as Henry Ward Ranger's solemn and moody brushwork gave way to the bright and broken colors of Childe Hassam.

Galleries on the second floor feature photographs, paintings, and sketches that fill in the details of the Old Lyme art colony. A large gallery building added to the property in 2002 exhibits some of the museum's rich holdings of Connecticut art.

For all her attention to her artists, Miss Florence did not neglect her gardens, where perennials, roses, vegetables, and herbs flourished in exuberant disarray. Painters still set up their easels to capture the grandmotherly mix of phlox, hollyhocks, and delphiniums basking in the seaside light.

After a dizzying two decades, the colony began to peter out and Miss Florence had few boarders. She still nurtured the local art scene as the first manager of the Lyme Art Association gallery, which opened next to her house in 1921, but she never seemed free of financial difficulty. In 1936, when artists learned that their onetime landlady was in danger of losing her home, they formed the Florence Griswold Association to buy the house and establish it as a museum. They lost out to a higher bidder, who allowed Miss Florence to stay in her family home until her death on December 6, 1937.

In writing of her death, the *New York Times* noted that "in her delicate and high-bred way, Miss Florence had her part in fostering an authentic American art." Several years later, the association succeeded in buying the house, which opened as a museum in 1947.

KATHARINE HEPBURN'S SEASIDE PARADISE
Katharine Hepburn Cultural Arts Center, 300 Main Street, Old Saybrook; 860-510-0473; katharinehepburntheater.org; see website for performance schedule. Katharine Hepburn Museum open Tuesday through Friday and one hour prior to all shows; free.

When Old Saybrook decided to restore a stately old building on Main Street to its original use as a theater, municipal officials didn't have to struggle to find a name. After all, how many towns of roughly 10,000 people can claim a movie star—one with four Academy Awards, no less—as one of their own?

Katharine Hepburn died in Old Saybrook on June 29, 2003, and did not see the opening of the Katharine Hepburn Cultural Arts Center in 2009. The roughly century-old red-brick neoclassical structure had been built for the Old Saybrook Musical and Dramatic Club. Over the decades, it was pressed into service as a basketball court and as town offices. Hepburn, no doubt, would have approved of its return to the performing arts.

Affectionately known as "The Kate," the center presents an ambitious schedule of mostly musical performances in its 260-seat theater and, of course, screens classic films. A small museum traces the life and impact of the actress whose off-screen personality was a match for the strong, independent women that she portrayed on stage and the silver screen. In the course of a six-decade career, she set a record for most best performance Oscars. She also received

Library of Congress

David Lyon

a Lifetime Achievement Award from the Fashion Designers of America in 1985 for pioneering a relaxed and self-confident style that helped to define the modern American woman.

Old Saybrook residents still relish their association with Hollywood royalty. But Hepburn returned their affection. Writing of Old Saybrook in her 1991 autobiography, *Me: Stories of My Life*, she declared, "To me it *is*—well, as I said paradise. I was and am nothing special here. I've been here since I was six."

One of six children, Katharine Hepburn was born on May 12, 1907, in Hartford, Connecticut. Her father, Thomas Norval Hepburn, was a physician; her mother, Katharine Houghton Hepburn, was actively involved in promoting women's rights, including the right to vote and access to birth control. Both parents encouraged their children to be independent thinkers.

The Hepburn family began visiting Old Saybrook in 1913. They purchased a waterfront 1870s house in the summer colony of Fenwick, popular with Hartford society for its proximity to the city and its location at the mouth of the Connecticut River where it flows into Long Island Sound. A self-described tomboy, Hepburn enjoyed idyllic summers swimming, playing golf and tennis, and engaging in all sorts of competitions, from diving contests to three-legged races.

When the house was destroyed in the Great New England Hurricane of 1938, the family rebuilt on the same spot the following year. Fenwick, as she called the home, always loomed large for Hepburn as a place to slip the demands and burdens of her life and career.

In 1928, Hepburn graduated from Bryn Mawr, a Pennsylvania women's college, with a degree in history and philosophy. Acting in school plays, not academics, set her on her career path. Although her father was initially opposed, likening acting to "a silly profession closely allied to streetwalking" (as she wrote in her autobiography), Hepburn forged ahead. After a number of appearances on Broadway, she made the leap from minor roles to the lead as the Amazon princess Antiope in *A Warrior's Husband*. The 1932 play caught the eye of film directors and took her to Hollywood.

Her first film, also in 1932, was *A Bill of Divorcement* with John Barrymore. As part of the RKO studio system, she made five more films between 1932 and 1934. Hepburn won her first Academy Award for the 1933 film *Morning Glory*, with Douglas Fairbanks, Jr. She also established her habit of not attending the awards ceremony.

Hepburn made little effort to fit the Hollywood starlet mold. For one thing, she was six inches or so taller than most leading ladies, carried herself with an athletic bearing, and spoke with a distinctive voice and accent. She also insisted on wearing slacks long before it became fashionable and didn't wear makeup unless she was in costume. She was reluctant to give interviews or pose for photos. Nevertheless, Hepburn charted a long career playing strong, self-assured women like herself.

David Lyon

That's not to say that she didn't endure ups and downs in a notoriously fickle industry. After a run of poorly received films in the late 1930s, Hepburn was deemed "box-office poison." Taking her career in her own hands, she returned to Broadway to star in *The Philadelphia Story*. The play was a smash hit. After securing the film rights, Hepburn returned to Hollywood to star in the 1940 film version, with Cary Grant and James Stewart.

Over the decades, Hepburn performed with practically every major leading man. But the 1942 film *Woman of the Year* with Spencer Tracy marked a turning point in her life. She had been married and divorced and had pursued other relationships, including a three-year affair with Howard Hughes, but she found her life partner in Tracy. Although he was married and never divorced, they were a couple until his death in 1967.

Popular at the box office, Tracy and Hepburn made eight more films together over the next twenty-five years. Hepburn also appeared with other leading men, including Humphrey Bogart in the 1951 film *The African Queen*, and received eight Oscar nominations between 1936 and 1963. It was her onscreen chemistry with Tracy in the 1967 film *Guess Who's Coming to Dinner* that resonated with Academy voters and earned her second win as leading actress. Hepburn claimed that she could never bring herself to watch it since Tracy died shortly after they finished filming.

She received her third Oscar for the 1968 film *The Lion in Winter*, with Peter O'Toole, and her fourth for the 1981 film *On Golden Pond*, with Henry and Jane Fonda. Hepburn's career slowed in her later years. In 1994, she appeared in the feature film *Love Affair* with Warren Beatty and Annette Bening and in the made-for-television movie *One Christmas*, based on an autobiographical short story by Truman Capote.

Hepburn divided her time between her townhouse in Manhattan and her Fenwick home in Old Saybrook. Her last lines in *One Christmas* might make a fitting epitaph: "I can sit back in my old age and not regret a single moment, not wish to change a single thing. It's what I wish for you . . . a life with no regrets."

HARRIET BEECHER STOWE'S FINAL HOME
**Harriet Beecher Stowe Center, 77 Forest Street, Hartford;
860-522-9258; harrietbeecherstowecenter.org; open year-round;
admission charged**

David Lyon

Harriet Beecher Stowe once wrote, "There is more done with pens than with swords." Her own life was proof of that adage. Her debut novel, *Uncle Tom's Cabin; or, Life Among the Lowly*, put such a human face on the horrors of slavery that Abraham Lincoln is said to have called her "the little woman who wrote the book that started this great war." The Lincoln tale might well be apocryphal, but it is true that Stowe's heart-wrenching depiction of enslaved people galvanized an international conversation about the moral depravity of slavery and clearly contributed to the climate in America that led to the Civil War.

Harriet was born on June 4, 1811, in Litchfield, Connecticut, where her father, the famed evangelist and social reformer Lyman Beecher, was serving as pastor of the

David Lyon

Congregational church. Beecher expected his children to be informed of the issues of the day and to engage in lively discussion around the dinner table. An ardent opponent of slavery, he encouraged his offspring to fight against injustice and for causes that they believed in.

Unlike most young women of her era, Harriet received an academically rigorous education, culminating in studies at the Hartford Female Seminary that had been founded by her older sister Catharine. Upon graduation, Harriet became a teacher at the school but focused principally on her writing. After winning a school essay contest at age seven, she made writing her chosen vocation.

When Lyman Beecher accepted the position of president of Lane Theological Seminary in 1832, Harriet and other family members moved west with him to Cincinnati. The city sat on the opposite bank of the Ohio River from the slave state of Kentucky, where Harriet was first exposed to an economic system built on slavery. She visited a plantation, where she saw firsthand the daily lives of enslaved people. Moreover, she met fugitives who had crossed the river to Cincinnati to escape bondage. As a Beecher, she was practically an abolitionist by birth, but seeing slavery in practice made her abstract opposition far more visceral. She was particularly horrified by the risks people had to take just to gain the freedom that was her birthright.

In 1836, Harriet married theology professor Calvin Stowe. Six of the couple's seven children were born before the Stowes moved to Brunswick, Maine, where Calvin joined the faculty at Bowdoin College in 1850. By the time she married, Harriet had published a geography book for children and a collection of short stories. But the book that would bring her literary immortality was yet to come.

In 1851, Harriet's personal life and national political tensions compelled her to "paint a word picture of slavery." Two years earlier, Harriet had lost her eighteen-month-old son, Samuel Charles, to cholera. Her own grief magnified her empathy for enslaved women who were forcibly separated from their children. She was also outraged by the Fugitive Slave Act that Congress passed in 1850. How could a moral nation impose fines and jail time on people—like Harriet and Calvin—who had aided enslaved people seeking freedom? How could it penalize those who had refused to assist so-called slave catchers?

Harriet proposed a three- or four-part series to run in the abolitionist newspaper the *National Era*. But it turned out that she had much more to say. More than forty chapters of *Uncle Tom's Cabin* were serialized between 1851 and 1852. When the chapters were gathered in a book in 1852, it marked the first time that an African American appeared as a main character in a major novel published in the United States.

The story of families torn asunder was at points melodramatic and sentimental, and the depiction of characters can seem insensitive and stereotypical to contemporary readers. For all of the book's shortcomings, it lit a fire in the public consciousness, galvanizing and polarizing American public sentiment about the shameful system. *Uncle Tom's Cabin* was also an instant international sensation. The book sold 10,000 copies in the first week it rolled off the presses. In the first year, it sold 300,000 copies in the United States. In Great Britain, it sold 1.5 million in a single year.

The *Sunday New York Times Book Review* quoted fiery abolitionist Frederick Douglass, himself escaped from bondage, proclaiming that Stowe had "baptized with holy fire myriads who before cared nothing for the bleeding slave." Stowe was as reviled in pro-slavery states as she was lauded by those drawn to the cause of abolition. Some parts of the South actually banned *Uncle Tom's Cabin*. Twentieth-century poet Langston Hughes called it "the most cussed and discussed book of its time."

Harriet did not return permanently to her native Connecticut until 1864, when Calvin retired from his professorship at Andover Theological Seminary in Andover, Massachusetts. They settled in the Nook Farm neighborhood of activists and reformers on the western edge of Hartford and oversaw construction of an elaborate Victorian Gothic home. When even America's best-selling author found it too expensive to keep up, the couple moved into a fourteen-room Victorian Gothic cottage in 1873. Harriet and Calvin's adult twin daughters, Hattie and Eliza, continued to live in the house until Harriet's death. The cottage is now part of the Harriet Beecher Stowe Center.

David Lyon

David Lyon

Although the home is largely furnished with pieces owned by Harriet or other family members, the tour focuses more on Stowe's achievements and sense of social justice than on the decorative arts and architecture of the Gilded Age. The dining room is set for a meal for six. The family relaxed in the back parlor with its modest piano and tufted Victorian sofa and entertained guests in the more formal front parlor—now set up to encourage discussions and debate among visitors on tour.

On the second level, the master bedroom is filled with heavy carved furniture in the American Empire style. A desk in one corner and a table by the window are covered with correspondence and manuscripts. It's a wonderfully messy vignette, complete with crumpled, rejected drafts overflowing onto the floor.

Harriet wrote in longhand with a flowing, urgent penmanship. By the time of her death on July 1, 1896, she had published more than thirty books, including fiction and poetry. She and her sister Catharine collaborated on *The American Woman's Home*, which, among other things, laid out a theory of scientific housekeeping and kitchen design. But it is her first novel, *Uncle Tom's Cabin*, that has made a lasting impact. In 2018, BBC Culture conducted a poll to identify works of fiction that "shaped mindsets or influenced history." The *Odyssey* by Homer received top billing, followed by *Uncle Tom's Cabin*, which was cited as "the first widely-read political novel in the US."

The Stowes at Bowdoin College

When the Stowe family lived in Brunswick, Maine, they rented the 1807 home at 63 Federal Street. When the rent proved to be a little steep for Calvin's salary as a professor, Harriet assured him that she could make up the difference with her writing. And write she did. It was here that she penned the book that attracted enthusiastic audiences when she read from the work in progress and ultimately propelled her to international fame.

The home is now owned by Bowdoin College, and much of it is dedicated to faculty offices. But one room, with a fireplace and windows facing the street, is set aside as "Harriet's Writing Room." Although it doesn't contain Stowe family possessions, its furnishings recall their time in the home. Visitors are welcome to peruse copies of *Uncle Tom's Cabin* and other books of that era and to read wall text that puts Harriet and her accomplishments into the context of her times. The room is open by chance.

PRUDENCE CRANDALL'S SCHOOL FOR YOUNG WOMEN

Prudence Crandall Museum, 1 South Canterbury Road, Canterbury; 860-546-7800; portal.ct.gov/ECD-PrudenceCrandallMuseum; open year-round; admission charged

Prudence Crandall didn't set out to become a hero when she opened a school for young women in Canterbury in 1831. But history sometimes has a way of setting the record

David Lyon

David Lyon

straight. In 1995, Connecticut named Crandall the State Heroine for demonstrating "great courage and moral strength by taking a stand against prejudice." Seventeen young women of African descent joined her in the struggle for educational equality.

Crandall was born in Hopkinton, Rhode Island, on September 3, 1803. Although her Quaker family moved to the small town of Canterbury in eastern Connecticut, Crandall was educated at the New England Friends Boarding School in Providence. Her intellectual grooming was rooted in the Quaker precepts of personal knowledge of the divine and a healthy skepticism of state-asserted authority.

Crandall was already an experienced teacher when she established the Canterbury Female Boarding School in 1831. The school occupied one of the finest Federal-style houses on the town green and educated the daughters of the town's most prominent families. It was off to a great start until Crandall admitted nineteen-year-old Sarah Harris as a day student in the fall of 1832.

Harris, the daughter of a local African American farmer, had already attended integrated school districts and studied alongside some of the girls who had become Crandall's pupils. She was keenly aware of the value of a good education. "Miss Crandall, I want to get a little more learning, if possible, enough to teach colored children and if you will admit me to your school, I shall forever be under the greatest obligation to you," Harris wrote. "If you think it will be the means of injuring you, I will not insist on the favor."

Harris was right when she predicted that her presence in Crandall's school would be met with resistance. Some families withdrew their daughters, and groups of influential citizens—first women, and then men—met with the teacher to point out the error of her ways. As all this was unfolding in Canterbury, Crandall was becoming increasingly aware of—and committed to—the abolition movement. She eventually traveled to Boston, where she was able to meet with one of the movement's leaders, William Lloyd Garrison. To help her to recruit new students, Garrison put Crandall in touch with preachers and other influential figures in free African American communities in the Northeast.

In the March 2, 1833, issue of Garrison's newspaper *The Liberator*, Crandall announced that "on the first Monday of April next, her School will be opened for the reception of young Ladies and little Misses of color. The branches taught are as follows: Reading, Writing, Arithmetic, English Grammar, Geography, History, Natural and Moral Philosophy, Chemistry, Astronomy, Drawing and Painting, Music on the Piano, together with the French language."

Crandall charged $25 per quarter for "board, washing and tuition." Her first out-of-state student arrived from Providence in April, and soon free Black middle-class families in Boston, New York, and Philadelphia sent their daughters to Canterbury to further their education.

Canterbury townspeople threatened Crandall with fines and, on at least one occasion, one of her students was threatened with a whipping. Undeterred, the young woman responded that she would take a whipping as long as she could get an education.

In mid-April, Crandall wrote to the Reverend S. S. Jocelyn in New Haven that "very true I thought many of the high-minded worldly men would oppose the plan but that Christians would act so unwisely and conduct in a manner so outrageously was a thought distant from my mind."

The conduct became even more outrageous in January 1834, when the school's well was polluted, a rock was thrown through a window, and a corner of the building was set on fire. Little damage was done because neighbors helped to extinguish the fire before it could spread to their homes.

Canterbury's leading citizens ultimately turned to the authority of the state to deter one teacher and her small group of students. With support from other towns, they petitioned the State General Assembly to forbid African Americans from other states to enter Connecticut for an education without the express consent of the town. Although the wheels of government often seem to turn painfully slowly, the so-called Black Law passed swiftly on May 24, 1833.

Crandall was arrested in June and spent a night in the county jail. She was tried twice and on October 3, 1833, was found guilty of violating the Black Law. Her case was appealed to the Connecticut Supreme Court of Errors in July 1834. Lawyer William Ellsworth argued that Crandall's students were citizens of their home states, noting that "a distinction founded in color, in fundamental rights, is novel, inconvenient, and impracticable." As citizens, he further reasoned, the young women had the right to pursue their education in Connecticut.

The court declared Crandall not guilty based on a technical error in her arrest warrant, but upheld the Black Law. Although Ellsworth did not prevail on the question of citizenship, he was one of the first to make an all-inclusive case for African American citizenship.

The Black Law was finally repealed in 1838, but by then it was too late for Crandall and her students. On September 9, 1834, a mob attacked the school, broke the windows, and threatened all within. The next day, Crandall closed the school rather than subject the young women to more danger.

That same year, Crandall married the Reverend Calvin Philleo and the couple left New England. Following Philleo's death in 1874, Crandall spent the remainder of her life on a farm in Elk Falls, Kansas, with her brother Hezekiah. She taught neighboring children in her home and continued to be a voice for human rights. She died on January 27, 1890. A historic marker in Elk Falls celebrates her accomplishments.

More than a half century after she was driven from her school, the state of Connecticut and the town of Canterbury made a formal written apology to Crandall and granted her an annuity of $400 per year. In 1969, the state purchased Crandall's former home and school and now operates it as a museum. Displays detail the history of what came to be called the "Canterbury Affair" and flesh out the continuing stories of the young women seeking to harness the power of education to improve their lives.

The museum also explores the impact of Crandall's case in the ongoing struggle for civil rights. In a blow to Crandall's beliefs, the Connecticut court's refusal to acknowledge that her students were US citizens was cited in the 1857 case *Dred Scott v. Sandford*. In that case, the US Supreme Court held that the US Constitution did not grant citizenship to African Americans. But the pendulum swung closer to justice in 1868 when the Fourteenth Amendment to the Constitution granted citizenship and equal protection of the law to all people—including the formerly enslaved—born or naturalized in the United States. William Ellsworth's argument echoes in the text of this crucial advance in civil rights.

Ellsworth's argument resonated again in 1954 when NAACP lawyer Thurgood Marshall cited the Crandall case as part of the background to his argument for equal rights in education in the case *Brown v. Board of Education of Topeka*. In a landmark ruling, the US Supreme Court declared that segregated public schools were unconstitutional.

But then, Prudence Crandall already knew that in 1832.

RHODE ISLAND

SARAH WHITMAN'S LITERARY HAVEN
Providence Athenaeum, 251 Benefit Street, Providence;
401-421-6970; providenceathenaeum.org; open year-round; free

Say the name Sarah Whitman and most people—if they recognize her at all—
immediately pair her with Edgar Allen Poe. That's a shame. Poe's romantic interest
was a fascinating and accomplished woman in her own right. In fact, that's why Poe
was attracted to her.

Sarah Helen Power was born in Providence on January 19, 1803. While she
spent most of her seventy-five years nurturing her own intellect and literary career,
her relationship with Poe lasted only a few fleeting months. Sarah began writing
poetry while she was still in school and began publishing her poems in newspapers
and magazines in the 1820s. She continued writing after her 1828 marriage to John
Winslow Whitman. The couple met while he was a student at Brown University
and they moved to Boston, where John Whitman practiced law and edited several
literary magazines.

David Lyon

After her husband's death in 1833, Sarah Whitman returned to Providence to live with her mother and sister in their family residence. The city would be her home for the rest of her life, and she quickly became a fixture in its intellectual and cultural scene. She was particularly drawn to the Providence Athenaeum, a member-supported library and cultural center founded in 1836. The Athenaeum moved into its temple-like Greek Revival building on Benefit Street in 1838, and it's not hard to imagine Whitman reading and writing in the double-height space where walls of books are punctuated by marble busts and statues.

Whitman moved in the same circles as many of the major writers and intellects of her day, including Ralph Waldo Emerson, Henry David Thoreau, Walt Whitman, and Margaret Fuller. Emerson's philosophical writings appealed to her since they reinforced her own inclinations toward self-reliance and independent thinking.

Whitman and Poe had not yet met when she wrote a poem as a tribute to him in early 1848. In it, she made reference to "The Raven," the narrative poem that had catapulted Poe to fame several years earlier. Poe, six years younger than Whitman, had also been widowed. They soon struck up a correspondence.

They first met in person when Poe traveled to Providence in September. The courtship quickly gained speed. When Poe was not visiting Whitman, letters flew between Providence and New York. In one, Whitman raised her concerns about their age difference, noting that "although my reverence for your intellect and my admiration of your genius make me feel like a child in your presence, you are not, perhaps, aware that I am many years older than yourself."

Poe responded by assuring her that "I truly, truly love you, and it is the most spiritual of love that I speak, even if I speak it from the depths of the most passionate of hearts."

The couple spent time in the Providence Athenaeum, where the intimate book-filled alcoves seem almost made for romantic trysts. They would also sometimes stroll in a local cemetery, and that is where Poe is said to have proposed marriage. Although both reportedly had misgivings—and Whitman's family was strongly opposed—Whitman and Poe planned to marry on Christmas Day 1848. Two days before the wedding, while sitting in one of the Athenaeum alcoves where they had spent so many happy hours, Whitman called off the wedding, perhaps out of concern over Poe's drinking.

Although Poe left Providence and the couple never saw each other again, their portraits hang in the Athenaeum's Art Memorial Room. Poe died less than a year later.

Whitman never married again, but she did come into her most productive years as a writer. She published her first book of poems, *Hours of Life, and Other Poems*, in 1853 and became a prolific essayist. Many of her essays were published in the *Providence Daily Journal* and reveal the workings of a lively mind. Whitman wrote criticism on literature and art, recounted her travels, and commented on politics, fashion, and architecture. She also frequently wrote in support of both feminism and Spiritualism, movements that appealed to the practical and visionary aspects of her nature, respectively. Visitors may make an appointment to see her books in the library's Rare Book Room.

Whitman played an active role in the struggle to secure legal and political rights—particularly suffrage—for women. In her poem "Woman's Sphere," which she read at a suffragist banquet in Providence in 1871, she tells women: "Better no more on flimsy fineries dote / But take the field and claim the right to vote."

Whitman was also acquainted with Andrew Jackson Davis, an early leader of American Spiritualism. Whitman embraced the belief that spirits of the dead can communicate with the living, often through the interventions of a medium, and may have held séances in her home. She maintained an interest in Spiritualism for the rest of her life and once even suggested in an essay that she had received messages from Poe.

Messages or not, the author and onetime suitor did remain a presence in Whitman's life. Convinced that early biographers had treated him unfairly, she worked to burnish his reputation. For the rest of her life, Whitman recounted her relationship with Poe to biographers seeking to paint a balanced portrait of his life. She also published her own book, *Edgar Poe and His Critics*, in 1860.

But in the end, she was most concerned with her own legacy. She left funds to publish another book of her poems after her death on June 27, 1878. *Poems of Sarah Whitman* appeared the following year.

In the Neighborhood

While you're in Providence, take the opportunity to see a notable work by Maya Lin (see page 7). Her sculpture *Under the Laurentide* is installed at the east entrance plaza of 85 Waterman Street on the Brown University campus.

ALVA SMITH VANDERBILT BELMONT'S NEWPORT MANSIONS

Marble House, 596 Bellevue Avenue, Newport; 401-847-1000; newportmansions.org; open year-round; admission charged

Belcourt Mansion, 657 Bellevue Avenue, Newport; belcourt.com; open year-round for weekend guided tours; admission charged

Even if you don't adhere to Marie Kondo's decluttering techniques or live in a "tiny house," it's almost impossible to imagine inhabiting one of the late nineteenth-century mansions that line Bellevue Avenue in Newport. These so-called cottages were built by some of the country's wealthiest families, who spared no expense in their efforts to impress—or outdo—their neighbors. Legendary socialite Alva Smith Vanderbilt Belmont actually managed to preside over not one, but two of these monuments to Gilded Age excess.

Alva's ascent to the upper rungs of society would make a good story in itself. But at midlife she reinvented herself as an avid suffragist, channeling her wealth, hard-won social position, and knack for throwing great parties into the cause of equal rights.

Her journey began in Mobile, Alabama, where she was born on January 7, 1853, into a distinguished southern family. Shortly after the Civil War, her cotton merchant father relocated his wife and three daughters to New York City. Before the family fell on hard times, Alva developed a taste for the finer things, including trips to Europe and occasional summers in Newport.

Alva secured her financial future in 1875 when she married William K. Vanderbilt, grandson of shipping and railroad magnate Cornelius Vanderbilt. But membership in one of the richest families in the country didn't open the doors to the upper echelons of Manhattan society. Led by Caroline Astor, gatekeeper to the elite, Manhattan's moneyed old families cast a cold eye on the "nouveau," no matter how "riche" they might be. Alva was not to be deterred. Legend has it that she schemed her way to the top after she and William moved into the Petit Chateau, their French

David Lyon

David Lyon

Renaissance–style mansion on Fifth Avenue that was completed in 1883. By hosting a lavish masquerade ball that Mrs. Astor could not afford to miss, the Vanderbilts' social standing was assured. The housewarming party was said to have cost $3 million and set a new bar for society galas.

The Petit Chateau was demolished in the 1920s, but two mansions in Newport still trumpet Alva's ambition and style. In the late nineteenth century, the most fashionable families often spent the summer in this posh community along Narragansett Bay. As a gift for Alva's thirty-ninth birthday, the Vanderbilts began construction of their own cottage. Whether by chance or design, it was located next door to Caroline Astor's Beechwood.

The Vanderbilts turned again to architect Richard Morris Hunt, who had designed the Petit Chateau and understood Alva's desire to cast herself, her husband, and their three children as American aristocracy. Completed in 1892, the fifty-two-room mansion was inspired by the Petit Trianon, the mini-palace at Versailles favored by Queen Marie Antoinette. It took no imagination to name it Marble House, since half a million cubic feet of the stone were used in the construction. Nearly two-thirds of the reported $11 million cost went into the white marble of the facade and the yellow and pink marble for the interior.

Alva hired a distinguished French interior decorating firm to create what was in essence a grand stage set where she would hold court as hostess. The Versailles-inspired dining room features a room-length table and heavy chairs that servants would pull out so that guests could be seated. The Gold Room is even more regal, with a crystal chandelier hanging from the mouth of Apollo and a bronze fireplace surround that replicates a statue by Michelangelo. Gold leaf covers nearly all the exquisitely carved woodwork.

With stained glass windows and a mock-cathedral fireplace, the Gothic Room was the perfect setting for William's collection of medieval armor. He occupied a fairly small bedroom where a desk overshadows the bed. Alva, on the other hand, luxuriated in a pinkish-lavender bedroom with an elaborately carved ceiling and silk brocade on the walls.

Alva only enjoyed Marble House for three years before she bucked social convention by refusing to turn a blind eye to William's philandering. Instead, she sued for divorce and exacted a handsome financial settlement, Marble House, and custody of sons William Jr. and Harold. Daughter Consuelo's marriage to the Duke of Marlborough helped Alva maintain her position in society.

David Lyon

Alva didn't waste much time before she married family friend Oliver Hazard Perry Belmont in 1896. When she moved a block down Bellevue Avenue to his fifty-room mansion, her work was cut out for her. Called Belcourt, the property had been designed by Richard Morris Hunt with sport, rather than entertaining, in mind. The ground floor featured a carriage room, stables, and a central marble trough for Belmont's horses. Alva evicted the horses and had the mansion remodeled to her taste. By all accounts, the couple led a contented, pampered life until Belmont's death in 1908. Since 2012, Belcourt has been owned by Rhode Island jewelry designer Carolyn Rafaelian (of Alex and Ani fame). She has underwritten a massive restoration of the property and has furnished it with her personal collection of Art Deco furniture.

After Belmont's death, Alva reopened Marble House. She was more than fifty years old and was poised to write a new chapter in her life. Inspired by lectures by early suffragists, Alva threw herself into the movement to secure voting rights for women and to advance the broader cause of equal rights. She was allied with several organizations and often spoke out for greater involvement of African American and working-class women. In New York, she supported female garment workers in the Triangle Shirtwaist Factory strike of 1909–10. The largest strike by women workers at the time, it led to better wages until it burned down in a fire on March 25, 1911.

Alva focused most of her energy on the National Woman's Party (NWP), which had been founded by New Jersey suffragist Alice Paul in 1916. The NWP's tactics, including lobbying Congress and organizing parades, suited Alva's own assertive approach to life. In January 1917, the NWP made history as the first organization to picket the White House.

Marble House wasn't entirely incompatible with Alva's new passion. She sponsored suffrage lectures and took full advantage of her social position to host fund-raising events and build support for the cause. She often courted wealthy donors in the marvelous caprice of a Chinese teahouse that she had built on the back lawn.

After the Nineteenth Amendment granting the vote to women was passed in 1920, Alva lived primarily in France. That same year, however, she was elected president of the NWP, a position she held until her death in 1933. The organization remained a voice for women's rights around the world and first proposed an Equal Rights Amendment to the US Constitution in 1923.

In 1929, Alva was instrumental in purchasing a historic home on Capitol Hill in Washington, DC, as the NWP's headquarters. Now an educational organization focused on promoting public understanding of the women's rights movement, the NWP still occupies that building. In 2016, President Barack Obama designated it the Belmont-Paul Women's Equality National Monument.

In the Neighborhood

While you're in Newport, take the opportunity to view two sites associated with Jacqueline Kennedy (see page 115). St. Mary's Church, where she and John Fitzgerald Kennedy were married, is located at 123 William Street. The site of their wedding reception, Hammersmith Farm, is at 225 Harrison Avenue.

DORIS DUKE'S NEWPORT MANSION
Rough Point Museum, 680 Bellevue Avenue; 401-847-8344; newportrestoration.org; open March through October and December; admission charged

A generous philanthropist throughout her life, heiress Doris Duke made her biggest impact on Newport, where she lived part of the year and launched an ambitious preservation foundation. Rough Point, her Newport summer "cottage," was just one of her five homes. She owned a Park Avenue penthouse in Manhattan, Duke Farms

David Lyon

(a 2,000-acre New Jersey estate), the phantasmagorical Shangri La (a palace inspired by Islamic art and culture near Diamond Head in Honolulu), and Falcon Lair (a Beverly Hills mansion originally built for Rudolph Valentino). But Newport may be the home where her legacy looms largest.

The daughter of tobacco magnate James Buchanan Duke and Nanaline Holt Inman, Doris Duke was born in New York on November 22, 1912. She grew up in a Fifth Avenue mansion and, as the only child of the founder of American Tobacco and Duke Energy companies, was soon dubbed "the richest little girl in the world."

In 1922, James Duke purchased Rough Point at the rocky tip of Aquidneck Island so the family could enjoy the social scene and cool breezes of Newport in the summer months. The home had been built between 1887 and 1891 for Frederick W. Vanderbilt and his wife, Louise. According to the *Newport Mercury*, it was the largest and most expensive house in the country at the time. That was saying a lot, given that it sits on Bellevue Avenue, the so-called Millionaires' Mile of opulent Gilded Age mansions. But thirty years later, James Duke went about modernizing and enlarging the house to meet his family's needs and to allow for the extravagant entertaining expected by their social set.

Alas, James Duke had little time to enjoy Rough Point before his death in 1925. He left most of his fortune to Doris, whose inheritance of $80 million was released in installments on her eighteenth, twenty-first, and twenty-fifth birthdays. Mother

David Lyon

and daughter continued to spend time at Rough Point until the grounds were damaged in a 1954 storm.

Doris came back in 1958. Having decided to donate her family's Manhattan mansion to New York University to house the Institute of Fine Arts, she needed someplace to put all the fine furniture, paintings, tapestries, porcelains, and other decorative arts that had filled the mansion. Rough Point was a natural choice. Duke transferred the art and furniture to the Newport property and spent time there between May and November for the rest of her life. There's no denying the grandeur of Rough Point, yet the most intriguing aspects of the property tours are the glimpses of the private life of the heiress.

Duke led a big and eventful life under the nearly constant glare of the media spotlight. She was married and divorced twice, and her romantic entanglements were the subject of gossip and speculation. Duke Kahanamoku, an Olympic gold medal swimmer, taught her to surf in the waters below Shangri La. He was also rumored to be her lover—as were other men as dissimilar as General George Patton and Marlon Brando. During World War II, Duke worked in Europe for the Office of Strategic Services, the predecessor of the Central Intelligence Agency. After the war she spent five years as the fashion editor of the Paris bureau of *Harper's Bazaar*. Duke collected art and antiques, cultivated and hybridized orchids, and studied belly dancing and modern dance. She sang in a Black gospel choir and studied jazz piano and composition. She was also known as a fashion icon. One room at Rough Point displays selections from her wardrobe.

But most of the mansion remains just as she left it, making it easy to envision how she lived here. The glittering 2,000-square-foot music room, which her father had added during the 1920s renovations, was the site of Duke's 1930 debutante party for 600 guests. Later in life, she held informal jam sessions around the baby grand piano. She hosted intimate dinner parties in the dining room before guests would retire to sit before the fireplace in the wood-paneled morning room. Duke was particularly fond of the small solarium where she could enjoy the ocean view through three walls of windows. She often ate her meals there. There's no record that she surfed the breakers at Easton's Beach, but she did swim off the rocks at the border of her property. When advancing age sapped her tolerance for the cold ocean water, she had a saltwater pool installed in the basement.

With stained glass windows and a procession of oversized oil portraits, the grand staircase could have been transported from a baronial manor. On the second floor, the family would relax in the Pine Room. Doris used the reel-to-reel tape recorder in the corner to capture herself and her friends singing and playing piano. Her rendition of a jazz standard floats through the air—her voice warm and clear and her phrasing reflecting her friendships with jazz musicians of the day. Also on the second floor, Duke's bedroom was her private sanctuary. Mother-of-pearl furnishings sit against yellow walls complemented by regal purple drapes. A painting by Renoir hangs over the fireplace.

Rough Point was often a place of rest and respite for Duke, but she could not escape media scrutiny when one of the most tragic incidents in her life took place here. On October 7, 1966, a rented car that Duke was driving struck and killed her friend and interior designer Eduardo Tirella when he left the vehicle to open the front gate. Police investigations concluded that it was an accident, but questions about the circumstances of the event still occasionally surface.

Duke took philanthropy seriously, donating the equivalent of more than $400 million in today's dollars during her lifetime. Many of her contributions were made anonymously. She supported historically Black colleges and universities, AIDS research, and Native American communities. Her concerns ranged from mental health and family planning to environmental conservation. Even with such generosity, at her death on October 28, 1993, Duke's estate was valued at $1.2 billion. The terms of her will established the Doris Duke Charitable Foundation and made provisions for Shangri La and Rough Point to open to the public as museums and for Duke Farms to serve as a center for environmental stewardship.

Duke made her largest philanthropic investment during her lifetime in Newport. Concerned that the city was sacrificing its unique architectural character to urban renewal and development, she founded the Newport Restoration Foundation in 1968. Jacqueline Kennedy Onassis (see page 115) was vice president and served on the board of directors until the early 1980s. Duke donated almost $22 million in funds and property to restore more than eighty eighteenth- and early nineteenth-century buildings. Recognized for its leadership in preserving early American architecture, the foundation remains the steward of one of the largest collections of colonial-era homes in the United States.

Focus on Newport Roots

Most of the properties owned by the Newport Restoration Foundation are rented to Newport residents, maintaining their original purpose as dwellings and contributing to the vibrancy of the city's historic neighborhoods. Two properties, however, are open to the public.

Housed in a redbrick 1811 home of a successful merchant, the Whitehorne House Museum displays eighteenth-century Newport-made furniture that remains highly prized for its fine craftsmanship and distinctive details. Located barely over the urban line in Middletown, forty-acre Prescott Farm recalls the area's agricultural roots. In addition to the original 1730s country house, Duke relocated several other historic buildings to the site. They include a more modest farmhouse of the same era and an early nineteenth-century windmill.

Visitors to Newport can also take in a major landscape installation by Maya Lin (see page 7). Also supported by the Newport Restoration Foundation, *The Meeting Room* at Queen Anne Square includes selected quotations from historic Rhode Island documents cut into the thresholds of the project's three building foundations.

See the Newport Restoration Foundation website for details.

PRINCESS RED WING'S MUSEUM

Tomaquag Museum, scheduled to move from 390A Summit Road, Exeter, to Ministerial Road, Kingston, in 2023; check website for details; 401-491-9063; tomaquagmuseum.org; open year-round; admission charged

Walter and Hannah Glasko's daughter was born on March 21, 1896, in Sprague, Connecticut. In keeping with state recording conventions, she was given the anglicized name of Mary Glasko. But her mother also gave her the traditional name of Red Wing. The intent was "to fling her mission far with grace, with ears that harken for the uplift of my race." Over time, Princess Red Wing became her preferred name.

Princess Red Wing was of Narragansett/Pokanoket-Wampanoag heritage. Her mother and her maternal grandmother filled her with the stories and legends of her people—a history passed on person by person from generation to generation. It became Princess Red Wing's lifework to preserve those oral tales and to share the history and culture of the Indigenous peoples of southeastern New England as widely as possible.

She tried to never miss an opportunity to dispel stereotypes about Indigenous people—or to celebrate the centuries-old cultural beliefs and customs. Beginning in the 1920s, she traveled throughout the United States to lecture at colleges and universities, a career she pursued for more than thirty years. She also held a seat on the Speaker's Research Committee of the Undersecretariat of the United Nations from 1949 to 1970.

"When you're the only Indian in the place," she later remarked, "they notice you." In fact, Princess Red Wing was always ready to provide an Indigenous perspective on a range of topics of global import and was a fierce defender of her people.

Most famously, she refused to take part in a ceremony at Mount Rushmore in the 1930s because the prepared script characterized the Indigenous peoples of New England as "dirty painted savages." Along with her firm refusal, she included a lesson

David Lyon

and some perspective, telling the sponsors "that they did not know their history of New England natives who, in that age of yore, jumped in the water every single morning to cleanse their bodies."

Princess Red Wing made perhaps her greatest impact close to home. In 1945, she became Squaw Sachem of the New England Council of Chiefs, an honored position that enabled her to preside over sacred ceremonies such as weddings, baptisms, and festivals of thanksgiving. As the bearer of Indigenous culture, she bestowed traditional names on countless children.

Princess Red Wing had a special commitment to young people. She spoke tirelessly at schools, libraries, and Scout meetings. For almost three decades, she gathered Scouts around campfires throughout New England to regale them with stories and legends of the people who first settled the region.

Princess Red Wing's legacy lives on in the Tomaquag Museum, which she cofounded in 1958 with her friend Eva Butler. An anthropologist, Butler had a large collection of Indigenous materials from throughout America and devoted part of her home to the museum. Princess Red Wing provided the history and perspective to put the artifacts into context and to bring Indigenous culture to life. The Tomaquag Museum was the first—and remains the only—Indigenous museum in Rhode Island.

Following Butler's death, the museum was relocated to Exeter and currently occupies a historic building that had served as a farmhouse and a church. Princess Red Wing continued to guide the museum until her death on December 2, 1987. As curator, she expanded the collections, adding materials from local Indigenous peoples as well as from throughout the Americas. She also established the educational philosophy of the museum by making it a living place where Indigenous history, culture, and traditions are celebrated and made relevant to contemporary life. In 1975, the University of Rhode Island recognized Princess Red Wing's commitment to her culture by awarding her a Doctor of Humane Affairs.

In 2016, the museum was awarded the National Medal for Museum and Library Service, which the Institute of Library and Museum Services describes as "the nation's highest honor for institutions that make significant and exceptional contributions to their communities." Established in 1994, the medal recognizes museums and libraries "that demonstrate extraordinary and innovative approaches to community service."

With plans for a new facility under way, the Tomaquag Museum is poised to expand that reach. The University of Rhode Island has entered into a partnership with the museum, which will construct a new complex of four museum buildings on an eighteen-acre parcel of university-owned land. The landscaping will lean heavily on herbs and plants associated with Indigenous culture.

Museum staff hope to move into their new quarters by fall 2023. It will be the latest step in furthering Princess Red Wing's lifelong commitment to preserving and sharing her culture. "My life work," she reflected in her later years, "has been to keep up the heritage of my people teaching it to all races and nationalities, and especially to youth."

EDITH WHARTON'S SUMMER HOME

The Mount, 2 Plunkett Street, Lenox; 413-551-5111;
edithwharton.org; open for guided and self-guided tours May through
October; admission charged

Once Edith Wharton put pen to paper, she couldn't stop writing. During her long career, she published more than forty books, most of them novels or novellas. In 1921, she became the first woman to be honored with the Pulitzer Prize for Fiction for *The Age of Innocence*, a novel that paints a less than flattering portrait of the upper-class Gilded Age society into which she was born.

Edith Newbold Jones came into the world in her family's Manhattan brownstone on January 24, 1862. Her mother was said to look and act like Queen Victoria, and her father was a scion of the wealthy, tradition-bound family that inspired the term "keeping up with the Joneses." That milieu would prove to be rich with subject matter. "Fate had planted me in New York," Wharton wrote in the April 1933 issue of the *Atlantic Monthly*, "and it was always my instinct as a story-teller to use the material nearest to hand, and most familiarly my own."

David Lyon

David Lyon

Edith spent much of her childhood in France, Italy, and Germany and was educated by tutors and governesses. Although she showed interest in writing as a child, little was expected of her, except to make a good marriage. She seemed at risk of becoming a spinster before she finally married Edward Robbins Wharton of Boston in 1885. Edith was twenty-three years old and "Teddy," as everyone called him, was more than a decade older. The couple traveled extensively and had homes in Manhattan and Newport, Rhode Island.

Breaking from the narrow role prescribed for women in her social class, Wharton published her first novel, *The Valley of Decision*, in 1902. She achieved literary acclaim three years later with *The House of Mirth*. The novel deftly combines a compelling tale and sympathetic heroine with a critical look at what Wharton herself described as "a society so relentlessly materialistic and self-serving that it casually destroys what is most beautiful and blameless within it."

Wharton was no less critical of the Gilded Age decorating style of overstuffed Manhattan townhouses and ostentatious Newport "cottages." In fact, her first book, written with architect Ogden Codman, Jr., was her definitive guide to style, *The Decoration of Houses*. More than a century after its publication, an *Architectural Digest* appreciation of Wharton noted that "all modern interior design books owe their existence to the pioneering guide that was all the rage in 1897." For those who prefer not to peruse the black-and-white photographs that illustrate the book, Wharton put her ideas into practice in the design of The Mount, her summer home in the Berkshires of western Massachusetts.

She purchased 113 acres in Lenox in 1901 and worked with Codman and fellow architect Francis L. V. Hoppin to realize her vision. With her taste honed in Europe, she created an English country estate with a French-style courtyard and Italianate terrace—a multinational synthesis of styles that somehow meshes perfectly. The property is by no means modest. The main house alone measures 16,850 square feet, yet embodies the sense of elegance and ease that Wharton craved.

She and Teddy lived at The Mount from May to October until 1911. Although the property is not furnished with Wharton family pieces, it nonetheless captures Edith's spirit and confident sense of style. The "wobbly velvet covered tables littered in geegaws . . . and festoons of lace on mantelpieces and dressing tables" that she railed against in *The Decoration of Houses* are nowhere to be found.

Wharton did nod to the Manhattan of her youth in the library on the main floor. Its carved walls and built-in bookcases were modeled after her father's library in her childhood home. "No children of my own age . . . were as close to me as the great voices that spoke to me from books," she wrote. "Whenever I try to recall my childhood it is in my father's library that it comes to life."

This clubby retreat seems the perfect space for a writer, but Edith favored her second-floor bedroom for her own literary endeavors. She wrote in bed every morning from sunrise until 11:00 a.m. Free from distractions (Teddy had a separate bedroom), she was able to complete *The House of Mirth* and *Ethan Frome*, which was published in 1911.

Wharton didn't like to throw grand parties, but she did enjoy entertaining friends such as sculptor Daniel Chester French, who had a summer studio in nearby Stockbridge, and Henry James. The writer once described The Mount as "a delicate French chateau reflected in a Massachusetts pond." The rooms at The Mount were arranged for quiet conversation and relaxation. Wharton preferred a round table in the dining room so that talk could flow freely. After dinner, guests would adjourn to the drawing room, where three separate seating areas invited more intimate chats. If the conversation lagged, they could step out onto the terrace at the rear of the house for a lively game of table tennis.

Or they might stroll in the gardens. In yet another book, the 1904 *Italian Villas and Their Gardens*, Wharton advised treating gardens as outdoor rooms, an approach she embraced at The Mount. Beautifully restored gardens on the property include an Italian walled garden, a formal French flower garden, an English-style meadow, terraced lawns, an allée of linden trees, and a kitchen garden designed by her niece, Beatrix Farrand (see page 179). Some of Wharton's beloved dogs, including Toto, Miza, and Jules, are buried in a graveyard on the property.

The Whartons sold The Mount in 1911 and divorced two years later. Edith made a fresh start in France and was living in Paris at the outbreak of World War I. She threw herself into humanitarian relief efforts and into reporting on the war from the front lines. In 1916, she was honored with the country's highest distinction, the French Legion of Honor.

She ultimately divided her time between Pavillon Colombe, an eighteenth-century home in the village of Saint-Brice-sous-Forêt on the northern outskirts of Paris, and Chateau Sainte-Claire, a restored convent in the south of France. Wharton left her old life behind. She returned to the United States only twice, making her last trip in 1923 to receive an honorary doctorate from Yale University.

Edith Wharton died at Pavillon Colombe on August 11, 1937, and is buried in Versailles. Yet she left a lasting mark in the Berkshires. The Mount, which Wharton called her "first real home," preserves her legacy and celebrates her as an independent spirit who burst the bonds of expectations for women of her age and class.

TINA PACKER'S SHAKESPEAREAN THEATER

Shakespeare & Company, 70 Kemble Street, Lenox; 413-637-3353; shakespeare.org; summer season late June through early October; admission charged

Shakespeare & Company set high artistic standards from the start. The company was only in its third season when *Village Voice* reviewer Terry Curtis Fox struggled to find adequate words to describe the way that Tina Packer's creative power unfolded

By Zachary deSilva, courtesy of Shakespeare & Company

David Lyon

on the stage. "Packer's production is a model of insight, clarity, vision," he wrote, before conceding that it was, "well, magic." But like all good magic, a lot goes on behind the curtain.

Founding artistic director Tina Packer launched Shakespeare & Company in the Berkshire Hills in 1978 with vocal coach Kristin Linklater and master teacher and actor Dennis Krausnick. Today the company is recognized as one of the largest and most respected Shakespearean festivals in North America.

Packer named the company for the bookstore that she had frequented during her bohemian days in Paris when she was fresh out of secondary school. She aimed high. Her goal was nothing less than to revitalize the Shakespeare canon by merging British actors' attentiveness to the spoken word with the physical energy and vitality of American actors.

Tina Packer was born on September 28, 1938, in Wolverhampton, England, and raised in Nottinghamshire. After her two-year adventure in France, she returned to England in 1962 and enrolled in the Royal Academy of Dramatic Arts. When she graduated two years later, she received an award for most promising actress. Within six months she had secured a three-year contract as an Associate Artist at the Royal Shakespeare Company in Stratford-upon-Avon.

Packer left the Royal Shakespeare Company before the end of her contract to take a lead in a fourteen-episode BBC television adaptation of Charles Dickens's *David Copperfield*, where she starred opposite Ian McKellen. She also continued to perform onstage and even played a love interest for Doctor Who in the cult-favorite BBC series. In 1971, she began teaching and directing at the London Academy of Musical and Dramatic Arts, where she directed *Measure for Measure* and *The Winter's Tale*.

By then, Shakespeare was in her blood. When Packer founded Shakespeare & Company, she had received several grants from the Ford Foundation to lay the groundwork for her innovative teaching methods and to travel the world to explore other traditions and approaches to acting and movement. The company settled in the Berkshire Hills, the state's summer arts capital, in 1978. The area boasts a supportive core of local arts lovers and draws both Bostonians and Manhattanites for its heady mix of dance, theater, music, and visual arts.

For more than two decades, the company was based at The Mount in Lenox, the former summer estate of Edith Wharton (see page 53). Packer's journey to The Mount and the company's persistence through early growing pains are captured in the 1985 book *Tina Packer Builds a Theater* by cultural reporter Helen Epstein.

The company kicked off its first season with *A Midsummer Night's Dream*. Since Wharton's mansion was then in disrepair and had no space large enough for a theater, the performance was staged outdoors. Actors flitted from the leafy edge of the surrounding forest to the lawns and bounded up the rear terrace. Audience members seated on the sloping lawn were charmed. A review in the *Berkshire Eagle* lauded the production for its "sheer, roistering energy," while noting that "there was not a pallid, pedantic moment during the entire evening."

Defying the weather, Shakespeare & Company continued to enchant audiences with season after season of outdoor performances. The physical grace of the actors and their fluid, natural ease with Elizabethan speech might look easy and effortless in performance, but such ease and grace flow only from untold hours of work and training. Those same qualities that set Shakespeare & Company apart in classic drama carry over into the contemporary plays that the company also mounts.

Shortly after that first summer season ended, the company established its other two signature programs. Shakespeare in the Schools brings the Bard to young audiences throughout the northeastern United States through workshops, residencies, and performances. The Center for Actor Training has helped hone the skills of countless professional actors from the United States and abroad.

Packer, who stepped down from her role as artistic director in 2009, has directed all of Shakespeare's plays at least once, performed in eight of them, and taught the Shakespeare canon at more than thirty colleges and universities. For four years, she taught in the MBA program at Columbia University, mining Shakespeare's plays for insights into modern-day issues in running a business. With faculty member John Whitney, she published *Power Plays: Shakespeare's Lessons in Leadership and Management* in 2001.

As eager to reach children as CEOs, Packer published *Tales from Shakespeare* in 2004 and received a Parents' Choice Award for her efforts to bring Shakespeare to new generations. Her decades-long study of the women in Shakespeare's plays led to the publication of *Women of Will: The Remarkable Evolution of Shakespeare's Female Characters* in 2016. It's also the title of the two-person stage piece that she has performed across the United States and abroad. In 2020, she published *Shakespeare & Company: When Action Is Eloquence* with actor, teacher, and writer Bella Merlin.

Packer is a recipient of the Commonwealth Award, the state of Massachusetts's highest honor in the arts. In 2019, she received a Lifetime Achievement Award from the Shakespeare Theatre Association for her unflagging commitment to bringing the works of Shakespeare to life for modern-day audiences and for nurturing successive generations of artists.

In 2000, Shakespeare & Company moved into its current home closer to downtown Lenox. The company now has its choice of five different theater spaces. Two outdoor venues recall the company's heady early days, while the tented outdoor Rose Footprint Theatre is a replica of the first level of Shakespeare's first theater in London. Of the two indoor theaters, the largest is appropriately named for the woman at the heart of the company. It is called the Tina Packer Playhouse.

SUSAN B. ANTHONY'S BIRTHPLACE
Susan B. Anthony Birthplace Museum, 67 East Road, Adams; 413-743-7121; susanbanthonybirthplace.org; open year-round; admission charged

It's easy to see why Massachusetts would want to lay claim to Susan B. Anthony. She certainly made history as one of the most influential and tireless leaders of the women's suffrage movement. Her base of operation might have been in New York, but she was born in a Federal-style home on the outskirts of the town of Adams in the Berkshire Hills. The property became a museum in 2010 and calls itself "the cradle of equal rights." An exhaustively researched guided tour makes the walls of the museum speak with uncommon eloquence.

The museum does not have any Anthony family artifacts, but three re-created rooms offer a sense of early nineteenth-century life, including a kitchen with a big fireplace for cooking and a small birthing room off the kitchen where Anthony was born on February 15, 1820. She was the second of seven children of Daniel and Lucy Anthony. Her father owned a cotton mill and also operated a general store in a large room at the front of the house. The store re-creation is filled with the kinds of goods that Daniel would have sold to neighboring farm families.

David Lyon

David Lyon

Celebrate

Susan B.
Anthony
Born 1820
Adams

David Lyon

Susan was only seven years old when her family moved to Battenville, New York, but she had already begun to absorb the teachings of her father's Quaker faith. The belief that all people are equal would be the foundation of her life's work. The Quaker practice of educating women and men equally would give her the tools she would employ as an activist for equal rights—a long career well documented by museum exhibits.

She studied to become a teacher in Philadelphia and taught for several decades, even as she became an activist and advocate for various social justice causes. By the late 1840s, Anthony was drawn to the abolitionist movement. By that time, her family had settled in Rochester, New York, and their home was a gathering place for activists including prominent abolitionist leaders Frederick Douglass and William Lloyd Garrison.

Although Anthony had previously been involved with the temperance movement, many women of her time first flexed their activist muscles in the fight to abolish slavery. It was, in some ways, a warm-up to the suffrage movement. In fact, Anthony first met Elizabeth Cady Stanton at an antislavery convention in Seneca Falls, New York, in 1851. They would work together for fifty years to advance the cause of equal rights. In 1863, the two women founded the Women's Loyal National League and collected almost 400,000 signatures on petitions to abolish slavery.

After the ratification of the Thirteenth Amendment in 1865 finally achieved that goal, Anthony and Stanton turned their attention to the cause of equal suffrage, reasoning that the most effective way to influence government was to exercise the right to vote. In 1866, they established the American Equal Rights Association to advocate for suffrage for all citizens of the United States, regardless of their race or gender. People of good intent on both sides soon split over whether or not to support the Fifteenth Amendment, which would grant African American men the right to vote.

In 1869, Julia Ward Howe, Lucy Stone, and Thomas Wentworth Higginson founded the American Woman Suffrage Association, which did support the Fifteenth Amendment and focused on gaining the vote for women at the state and local levels, arguing for a separate campaign for federal suffrage. On the other hand, Anthony and Stanton opposed separating the struggle for voting rights in a way that would leave women no closer to the ballot box. That same year they formed yet another organization, the National Woman Suffrage Association, to advocate for a constitutional amendment that would guarantee women the right to vote.

The Fifteenth Amendment was ratified in 1870—leaving behind women of all races. Two years later, Anthony made one of her boldest moves. In an effort to bring the issue of women's suffrage before the US Supreme Court, she marched into the polling place in Rochester and voted in the 1872 presidential election. She was arrested and brought to trial, where the judge told the jury to render a verdict of not guilty, but still fined her $100. Anthony refused to pay, expecting to appeal the decision all the way to the Supreme Court. But because the lower court did not enforce the fine, she did not suffer damages and therefore could not mount an appeal.

In 1890, the two suffrage organizations joined forces to create the National American Woman Suffrage Association. For the next decade, Anthony would serve first as vice president and then as president of the largest suffrage organization in the country and the leader in the fight for the vote. To say that she worked tirelessly is an understatement. She was always on the go, traveling around the country to give speeches, gather signatures on petitions, and lobby the US Congress. As passionate and indefatigable as she was, she was met with fierce opposition, ridicule, and misogynistic epithets.

"I have encountered riotous mobs and have been hung in effigy," Anthony once recounted, "but my motto is: Men's rights are nothing more. Women's rights are nothing less."

She continued her fight for justice to the end. Addressing a gathering of suffragists at a celebration of her eighty-sixth birthday in Washington, DC, she effectively passed the torch to a new generation. She told the women, "Failure is impossible!" She died shortly after on March 13, 1906.

US Mint

A full century after Anthony's birth in Adams, women finally won the right to vote when the Nineteenth Amendment was ratified on August 18, 1920. To this day, it is known as the Susan B. Anthony Amendment.

Coin of the Realm

Susan B. Anthony was the first female historical figure to be honored on a circulating coin from the United States Mint. The Susan B. Anthony Dollar was issued from 1979 to 1981 and then again in 1999. But the one dollar coin—roughly the size of a quarter—did not catch on with the American public. With relatively few coins issued, Anthony's profile portrait is now a favorite with collectors.

EMILY DICKINSON'S FAMILY HOME

Emily Dickinson Museum, 280 Main Street, Amherst;
413-542-8161; emilydickinsonmuseum.org; open March through
December; admission charged

Emily Dickinson wrote roughly 1,800 poems, touching on everything from the slant of light flowing through a windowpane to meditations on immortality. Yet, for someone who had so much to say, she remains the mystery woman of American poetry. Ever elusive, she is nonetheless a founding mother of American verse and a touchstone of American female identity.

Courtesy of Amherst College Archives & Special Collections

Emily was born on December 10, 1830, to Emily Norcross Dickinson and lawyer, politician, and civic leader Edward Dickinson. The middle of three children, she spent her early years in the Homestead, the 1813 home built for her paternal grandfather, Samuel Fowler Dickinson. In time, she and the yellow brick house would become inseparable.

Dickinson's family and community valued education. Her grandfather had been one of the founders of Amherst College. After several years studying in the local public school, Dickinson attended the private Amherst Academy from 1840 to 1847 and enjoyed lectures at Amherst College. She also spent the 1847–48 academic year at the relatively new Mount Holyoke Female Seminary (now Mount Holyoke College) in nearby South Hadley.

Her sojourn at Mount Holyoke marked the longest period that Dickinson spent away from her family home. But she was hardly a recluse as a young woman. She and her younger sister Lavinia spent time with acquaintances in Springfield, Massachusetts, and traveled to Philadelphia and Washington, DC, when their father was elected to the US Congress in 1853.

Edward Dickinson's reelection bid failed, and in 1855 he and his wife and two daughters returned to the Homestead, where they would all live for the remainder of their lives. Emily's brother Austin, who married one of her closest friends, Susan Huntington Gilbert, built an Italianate-style home next door, which they called The Evergreens. Austin and Susan made their home the epicenter of Amherst cultural and social life. Both the Homestead and The Evergreens are open to Emily

Courtesy of Emily Dickinson Museum

Dickinson Museum visitors via guided tours, and the two homes reflect the furnishings and lifestyles of the distinct members of the Dickinson family.

Emily Dickinson was apparently little interested in most domestic tasks or in the social obligations that came with her father's standing in the community. She did enjoy baking and gardening, but by her early twenties was increasingly drawn to writing. Once the family had settled back in the Homestead, she began her most productive period, which scholars define as the years from 1858 to 1865.

She often wrote at a small table in her bedroom at the southwest corner of the second floor. The room features lively floral wallpaper and a mannequin clad in Dickinson's simple white housedress. But she also wrote in the dining room, in the conservatory, or in the kitchen where she might jot thoughts on the back of a recipe or piece of wrapping paper.

That seven-year burst of creativity produced a startling body of work. By age thirty-five, Dickinson had composed more than 1,100 lyric poems notable for both their concision and their power. She tackled the hard subjects of human emotions—pain, grief, joy—and the leading metaphysical preoccupations of her era, notably Nature and eternal questions about the relation of Beauty and Art. She assembled about 800 of her poems in little sheaves of pages that archivists call fascicles. About forty of these booklets—resembling what modern poets might call chapbooks—survive.

By the time she reached her midthirties, Dickinson rarely ventured beyond her family compound on Main Street at the corner of Triangle Street. It was world enough for her far-ranging mind and soaring imagination. Dickinson cultivated lively, albeit primarily written, relationships with a wide circle of family members, friends, and literary figures such as Samuel Bowles III, editor of the *Springfield Daily Republican*, and author Thomas Wentworth Higginson, who was closely associated with the *Atlantic Monthly*. In 1869, Dickinson wrote to Higginson that "a letter always feels to me like immortality because it is the mind alone without corporeal friend." She often enclosed poems along with her letters. Some of those letters suggest that Dickinson had at least two serious romantic relationships.

Sister-in-law Susan Dickinson was the recipient of many of Emily's poems. When Emily died on May 15, 1886, Susan wrote a moving obituary for the *Springfield Daily Republican*: "Her swift poetic rapture was like the long glistening note of a bird one hears in the June woods at high noon, but can never see."

After her death, Dickinson's family discovered the sheer volume of her literary opus. In all, Emily Dickinson wrote about 1,800 poems. Only a single letter and ten poems are known to have been published during her lifetime. The poems were not attributed to her and were likely printed without her permission.

Emily's sister Lavinia was the first to determine that the poems deserved a greater audience. Her instincts proved correct. When *Poems of Emily Dickinson* was published in 1890, it met an eager reading public, going through eleven editions in less than two years. *Poems of Emily Dickinson, Second Series* followed in 1891, and *Poems of Emily Dickinson, Third Series* appeared in 1896.

As interest in both Dickinson's work and her private life grew, other publications of her poems and letters followed. *The Poems of Emily Dickinson*, published in 1955, was the first to collect most of her poems and to begin the long process of restoring them to more accurately reflect the way Dickinson had written them. Earlier editors had taken sometimes extreme liberties to make her idiosyncratic punctuation conform to literary norms. They also added titles and changed words in misguided efforts to smooth the diction or make the poems more accessible.

The editions that restore Dickinson's original forms are revelatory. They show a wide-ranging creative mind exploding literary conventions to push the limits of expression. Clearly Dickinson understood and respected formal poetic structure, yet felt free to defy its restrictions. Her wordplay can be scintillating, and her line breaks were a century ahead of her time as a means of scoring the reading of her poems. She interjected dashes to indicate a rhythmic pause and used capitalization for emphasis. Yet the careful reader soon capitulates to Dickinson's quirks, for they reveal the ravenous mind behind the verse.

The intimacy of her work—many readers liken it to a private conversation—continues to resonate. In her Nobel Lecture, Louise Glück, recipient of the 2020 Nobel Prize in Literature, fondly recalled, "I read Emily Dickinson most passionately when I was in my teens. Usually late at night, post-bedtime, on the living room sofa..."

Dickinson's appeal is hardly limited to writers. The poet is one of the thirty-nine women featured most prominently in the place settings of Judy Chicago's *The Dinner Party*, a watershed work of feminist art created between 1974 and 1979. A guest of honor at what would have been one the most fascinating of gatherings, Dickinson is seated between Elizabeth Blackwell, the first woman to receive a medical degree in the United States, and Ethel Smyth, an English composer and suffragist.

Three decades after Chicago's series, photographer Annie Leibovitz opened her book *Pilgrimage* with photographs of the Dickinson homes and of Emily's pressed herbs and white dress. Dickinson was, Leibovitz explained, the favorite poet of her longtime partner, writer and critic Susan Sontag.

Emily Dickinson's life was precisely the antithesis of today's media-driven culture, yet, in a universe imbued with metaphysical irony, the AppleTV+ series *Dickinson* became a hit with critics and viewers alike. In her early twenties, series creator Alena Smith, an author and screenwriter, had become fascinated with Dickinson.

"She was a true weirdo outsider artist," Smith says, "who reinvented the rules of poetry and managed to contain infinitely huge ideas on miniature scraps of paper."

CLARA ENDICOTT SEARS'S MUSEUM
Fruitlands Museum, 102 Prospect Hill Road, Harvard; 978-456-3924; thetrustees.org/place/fruitlands-museum; grounds open year-round, all museums except Art Museum closed in winter; admission charged

When Clara Endicott Sears built a summer home on Prospect Hill overlooking the Nashua River valley in 1912, she probably had no idea that she would be so drawn to the land and its people that she would be compelled to preserve their heritage. Nearly fifty years old, she was about to become a key figure in the nascent, largely male-dominated field of historic preservation.

Sears was born in Boston on December 16, 1863, into a wealthy old family that could trace its roots back to the first governor of the Massachusetts Bay Colony. Well educated in history and literature and widely traveled in Europe, she preferred an independent life over the prospect of marriage. She found her calling in the green, rolling farmlands west of Boston. Her estate eventually grew to 450 acres and included a working dairy farm as well as the site of the transcendentalist community established in 1843 by Amos Bronson Alcott and Charles Lane.

Fruitlands, as Alcott and Lane called their well-intentioned but ultimately ill-conceived experiment in self-sufficient communal living, lasted less than a year. But the 1820s farmhouse that had served as its base was still standing when Sears acquired the property. That single red building became the nucleus for a cluster of museums that Sears created.

David Lyon

David Lyon

Even with her extensive experience of Europe, Sears had a strong interest in matters close to home—especially New England history. She realized that she could preserve an important cultural and historical artifact of transcendentalism, America's homegrown philosophical movement grounded in progressive social views. She sought guidance from the Massachusetts Historical Society and the recently formed Society for the Preservation of New England Antiquities (now Historic New England). Having also acquired some of the original Alcott family furnishings from their brief sojourn here, she opened Fruitlands Farmhouse as a museum in 1914. She was just getting started.

The original Fruitlands utopian experiment under Alcott and Lane drew much of its inspiration from the Shakers. The transcendentalist founders were in close communion with the Shaker settlements in nearby Harvard and Shirley, which had been founded a half century earlier. Sears, too, took an interest in those Shaker communities, which were already in their final days. The celibate religious group had steadily declined in members in the decades after the Civil War as economic opportunity expanded and many New Englanders moved west. The Harvard Shakers formally closed in 1918, but not before securing Sears's commitment to help preserve their history.

The Shakers themselves disassembled the 1794 Trustees Building—essentially the gateway between their insular society and the outside world—and reassembled it plank by plank on Sears's property. Following restoration, the modest

one-and-a-half-story structure opened in 1922 as the world's first museum dedicated to the Shaker faith and lifestyle. Among its treasures is a Windsor-style rocker that belonged to Shaker founder Mother Ann Lee. The museum was also an early example of the practice of relocating threatened buildings of historic importance to another site.

When Native American arrowheads were uncovered on the Fruitlands property, Sears pondered how she could interpret the artifacts to illuminate how people lived on the land before the arrival of settlers from European stock. To reflect the original inhabitants—as well as Native American arts and cultures more broadly—she sought the assistance of experts at the Peabody Museum of Archaeology and Ethnology at Harvard University. Buying locally and by mail, she assembled a collection of Native American artifacts to document New England tribes as well as the Indigenous peoples of the Plains, Southwest, and Northwest. Her Native American Museum opened in 1928.

Harvard experts also offered advice when Sears began to collect early nineteenth-century folk portraits, before such "primitive" pieces were recognized by the arts establishment. She eventually assembled one of the largest collections in the world. Those portraits of New Englanders posing stiffly for itinerant artists greeted visitors in the Art Museum when it opened in 1939. The paintings caught the attention of another noted collector and researcher, Nina Fletcher Little (see page 118). She wrote, "There, for the first time in New England, a permanent museum collection displayed to the public a large group of controversial pictures that had recently been brought out of hiding in local attics and barns." Sears later built an addition to the museum so she could display her collection of Hudson River School landscape paintings.

Fruitlands has kept up with more-contemporary museum practices, reinterpreting the Native American Museum and the Art Museum. Curators often invite contemporary artists to provide fresh context in exhibitions that also draw on many of the materials from the museums' permanent collections. Similarly, contemporary artists provide pieces that augment the main historical collections of the Farmhouse and the Shaker Museum.

Sears also found time to write. Between 1918 and 1930, she published three historical novels set in the town of Harvard. But much of her work paralleled her commitment to preserving the stories of the people and places that had captured her imagination. Her titles include *Bronson Alcott's Fruitlands* (1915), *Gleanings from Old Shaker Journals* (1916), *Some American Primitives: A Study of New England Faces and Folk Portraits* (1941), and *Highlights Among the Hudson River Artists* (1947).

Accomplished in many fields, Sears also designed her country home, The Pergolas, in the style of "a villa with English comforts" and accentuated her gardens with columns and other artifacts that she imported from Italy. Ironically, the house was torn down after her death on March 25, 1960. But long before then, she secured her legacy by incorporating the Fruitlands Museum in 1930. In addition to the museum buildings and a café, the grounds offer more than two miles of hiking trails through the countryside that gave Sears such inspiration and pleasure.

LOUISA MAY ALCOTT'S FAMILY HOME
Orchard House, 399 Lexington Road, Concord; 978-369-4118; louisamayalcott.org; open year-round; admission charged

Louisa May Alcott was thirty-five years old when her publisher suggested that she write "a girl's story." She wasn't necessarily excited about the project, confiding in her journal that she "never liked girls, or knew many except for my sisters." That was enough. She reached back to her girlhood years to imagine the March family of *Little Women* as only thinly disguised versions of herself, her three sisters, their father, and their beloved mother, "Marmee."

Once she set her mind to it, Louisa wrote the 134,000-word first part of the novel in longhand between May and July 1868. In an era when boys' adventure stories were the mainstay of juvenile fiction, *Little Women* was eagerly received from the outset. Countless young girls felt a connection to the March sisters, especially headstrong tomboy Jo March, Louisa's spunky fictional counterpart.

David Lyon

David Lyon

More than 150 years later, the March family's story still resonates. "When I was young, I really identified with *Little Women* . . . particularly the character of Jo," Hillary Rodham Clinton told eleven-year-old interviewer Marley Diaz during the 2016 presidential campaign. "I remember reading that book and thinking, 'I want to be like that when I grow up.'" She was hardly alone. Women writers from Doris Lessing and Margaret Atwood to Anne Tyler, Barbara Kingsolver, and Jhumpa Lahiri all cite Jo March as an inspiration.

Little Women is set at Orchard House, the eighteenth-century property just outside Concord center that Amos Bronson Alcott bought for his family in 1857. A philosopher and educational reformer, Bronson was not much of a breadwinner. As he struggled to make a living, the family moved more than twenty times before finally settling in Concord.

Louisa was born on November 29, 1832, in Germantown, Pennsylvania. She was only two when the family returned to New England, living first in Boston. Bronson was part of the transcendentalist movement centered around Ralph Waldo Emerson and his home in Concord. In fact, Louisa's education almost reads like a master's seminar in transcendentalism. Although her father took the lead in educating his daughters, Louisa spent many an hour in Emerson's library and went on nature walks with Henry David Thoreau.

Louisa began writing poems, short stories, and theatricals almost as soon as she could grasp a pen. By the time she was fifteen, she was also helping to support her family, often working as a teacher, governess, or seamstress. But writing was her true calling and she published her first book, a collection of short stories called *Flower Fables*, in 1854. She also wrote popular potboilers, such as *Pauline's Passion and Punishment*, under the pen name A. M. Barnard. Louisa garnered national attention after the 1863 publication of *Hospital Sketches*, based on her experiences in Washington, DC, as a Civil War nurse. Although she served only a couple of months before becoming seriously ill with typhoid fever, her book helped to call attention to the poor condition of military hospitals.

David Lyon

David Lyon

Louisa had a long recuperation back at Orchard House, where the family lived until 1877. In the early twentieth century, the Concord Women's Club spearheaded the purchase of the property, which opened as a museum in 1912. About 80 percent of the furnishings are from the Alcotts and reflect the warmth of a settled family life and their rising fortunes as Louisa's literary success—especially *Little Women*—made the Alcott family financially secure.

Tours of the house begin in the kitchen and move quickly to the dining room and parlor, where the young women would perform Louisa's theatricals. The dining table is set with an embroidered cloth, fine china, and glassware. The melodion at the foot of the stairs belonged to Elizabeth (Beth in the novel), who died shortly before the Alcotts moved to Orchard House.

Anna Alcott (Meg in the novel) married John Bridge Pratt in the parlor in 1860. The two met when they performed together in a play at the Concord Dramatic Union, which Louisa and Anna had helped establish. The fictionalized account of the wedding ceremony has proven so romantic that men have been known to bring their girlfriends to Orchard House for surprise proposals.

May Alcott (Amy in the novel) was a talented artist. Louisa's support for her studies in Paris, London, and Rome helped bring her childhood dreams into an adult career. Even when they were growing up, May treated the plaster walls of her long, narrow bedroom as a canvas. Subsequent restoration has uncovered her images of Roman and Greek figures, chariots, mothers and children, and angels.

For most visitors, Louisa's big bedroom at the front of the house is the highlight of the tour. Between the two windows looking out on the main road, Bronson built a small semicircular desk so that his daughter would have a place to write. It's almost possible to imagine her pulling up a chair, picking up a pen, and writing, *"Christmas won't be Christmas without any presents,"* grumbled Jo, lying on the rug. *"It's so dreadful to be poor!"* sighed Meg, looking down at her old dress.

Louisa once declared, "I'd rather be a free spinster and paddle my own canoe." She remained true to her word and never married. Before her death on March 6, 1888, she cared for her mother and father, traveled in Europe, advocated for abolition and women's rights, and was the first woman to register to vote in municipal elections in Concord. She wrote more than thirty books and short story collections. But her legacy was already secure with *Little Women*—a book that has never gone out of print and has been translated into more than fifty languages.

In the preface to a 2018 edition, writer and punk rocker Patti Smith summed up the book's enduring appeal: "Louisa May Alcott wrapped herself in her glory coat, labored at her own desk, and penned a new kind of heroine. A stubbornly modern nineteenth-century American girl. A girl who wrote. Like countless girls before me, I found a model in one who was not like everyone else, who possessed a revolutionary soul yet also a sense of responsibility. Her dedication to her craft provided my first window into the process of the writer and I was moved to embrace this vocation as my own."

Concord's Literary Resting Ground

Located a short distance from Concord center, Sleepy Hollow Cemetery is a mecca for fans of American literature. The burial ground was dedicated in 1855 in a ceremony in which Ralph Waldo Emerson waxed eloquent. In 1888, he joined his old friend Henry David Thoreau on the high ground now called Author's Ridge. Nathaniel Hawthorne and his wife Sofia are buried there as well. The Alcott clan, including father Bronson and daughter Louisa May, are remembered by a line of stones on the right near the top of the ridge. Louisa's grave is often marked with a flag for her service as a Civil War nurse.

ALICE LONGFELLOW'S FAMILY HOME
Longfellow House–Washington's Headquarters National Historic Site, 105 Brattle Street, Cambridge; 617-876-4491; nps.gov/long; open late May through October; free

Alice Mary Longfellow was only ten years old when she became forever saddled with the sobriquet "Grave Alice." That's how her father, Henry Wadsworth Longfellow, described her in his 1860 poem "The Children's Hour." The verses paint a loving family scene as Alice and her younger sisters ("laughing Allegra" and "Edith with golden hair") plot to surprise their father in his study. Alice Longfellow spent her entire life in that home with its "broad hall stair," forging her own identity in the shadow of her famous father, a distinguished Harvard professor who retired from academia to become the most popular writer of his day.

The fine Georgian home was built in 1759 along a stretch of Brattle Street known as "Tory Row." Its wealthy owner, John Vassall, a loyal supporter of the British king, took his wife and children back to England in 1774 on the eve of the American Revolution. In 1843, Henry and his bride, Frances "Fanny" Appleton, received the home as a particularly nice wedding gift from Fanny's wealthy father, Nathan Appleton.

Alice was born in the home on September 22, 1850. She was the couple's third child and first daughter. By 1855, Alice had two younger sisters. Fanny took an

David Lyon

active role in the education of her children. Alice was taught by governesses and also attended Miss C. S. Lyman's School and Professor Williston's School. Fanny took great pains to chronicle each child's milestones and noted that Alice "likes to pick up a book & read stories & says more cunning things than can be remembered."

Alice's lifelong interest in history was no doubt fostered by her family's pride in their home's association with George Washington. When he assumed command of

the newly formed Continental Army, the general made the vacant Vassall mansion his home and headquarters from July 1775 until March 1776. Alice's fascination with Washington continued throughout her life. In 1879, she was elected as a member of the Mount Vernon Ladies Association, which acquired the first president's Virginia property in 1858 and has maintained it ever since. Alice assumed the task of repairing and furnishing the study at Mount Vernon. She used her own funds to purchase the secretary bookcase that Washington had used both during and after his presidency. The association considers it one of the most important pieces in their possession.

But Alice was most concerned with the Longfellow legacy. In 1913, she and other family members established the Longfellow Trust to preserve the family home in honor of her father. Alice lived in the Brattle Street manse until her death on December 7, 1928. Over the years, she restored the formal gardens on the property and modernized the bathrooms. Otherwise, she kept the home as it had been during the years when everyone from Ralph Waldo Emerson and Charles Dickens to Oscar Wilde and "Swedish Nightingale" Jenny Lind came to visit her father in his study and library. The portrait of young Alice and her two sisters that often illustrated "The Children's Hour" hangs in the dining room. Alice had her own spacious study and bedroom on the upper floor.

In 1917, Alice's nephew, Henry Wadsworth Longfellow "Harry" Dana, moved into the house and joined his aunt in the preservation effort. The pair worked to archive all the objects in the house—from letters and journals to such everyday items

David Lyon

as socks and spoons and a recipe for apple pie. One of the best-documented historic homes in the country, the Longfellow House opened to the public in 1930 and was donated to the National Park Service in 1972.

But Alice made perhaps her greatest contribution in the field of education, cofounding the Society for the Collegiate Instruction of Women, the forerunner of Radcliffe College, in 1879. Alice was a special student in the first class of women to be taught by Harvard professors. She continued to take classes for about a decade and hosted some of the early commencement ceremonies in the library of Longfellow House. At the same time, she helped guide the fledgling institution by serving as a member of the board of trustees and as the society's treasurer. In recognition of her unwavering support of women's education, Longfellow Hall, now part of the Harvard Graduate School of Education, was named in her honor.

How She Rolled

Alice Longfellow loved to travel. She first toured Europe with her family when she was in her teens and returned repeatedly as an adult. She was particularly fond of France and Italy. In 1913, while on a two-year European tour with her chauffeur, maid, and a niece, she purchased a custom Rolls-Royce 40/50 Silver Ghost. It was shipped to her in Florence, Italy, and she soon wrote to her sister

Edith that her new automobile "runs like a dream so far as noise, with a long flexible spring that rides the roughnesses like a canoe." When she left Europe in August 1914, she arranged to have the Rolls-Royce shipped to the United States. Alice owned the car for the rest of her life. It now resides in the collection of the Owls Head Transportation Museum (owlshead.org) in Owls Head, Maine.

JULIA CHILD'S GASTRONOMIC HAUNTS
Savenor's Butcher Shop and Market, 92 Kirkland Street, Cambridge; 617-576-6328; savenorsmarket.com; open year-round

Harvest, 44 Brattle Street, Cambridge; 617-868-2255; harvestcambridge.com; open year-round

It's too bad that the title *Joy of Cooking* was already taken when Julia Child burst into American kitchens in the 1960s. Child—who would go on to write a slew of cookbooks by other titles—did indeed radiate joy for the art of cooking and for sharing food with others. That pure enthusiasm would make her a culinary superstar.

Certainly no one knew that they would be seeing the birth of a cultural phenomenon when Julia Child was booked as a guest on the rather highbrow television show

Photograph W539622_81 by Paul Child. © Schlesinger Library, Harvard Radcliffe Institute

I've Been Reading in February 1962. Hosted by Boston College English literature professor P. Albert Duhamel, the show was a staple of Boston's fledgling WGBH educational television station.

Duhamel had interviewed a lot of authors, but Child was the first to arrive on the set with a big copper bowl, a balloon whisk, an omelet pan, and a hot plate. Her longtime producer Russell Morash later recalled thinking, "Who is this madwoman cooking an omelet on a book-review program?" But Child was on a mission to promote *Mastering the Art of French Cooking*, which had been published just a few months earlier.

"I thought it would be nice if we made an omelet," she told the host. "They're so delicious and easy to make."

Duhamel and the show's audience members could later claim bragging rights as witnesses to culinary history. In today's seemingly nonstop world of food shows, food channels, food bloggers, cooking competitions, and celebrity chefs, it's almost impossible to imagine the sensation caused by Child's little omelet. A couple dozen viewers reached out and asked for more, and Julia Child was on her way to changing how Americans cooked and ate. Arguably, she may have also launched our national obsession with food.

Child was almost fifty years old and had arrived at her moment via a circuitous route. She was born Julia Carolyn McWilliams on August 15, 1912, in Pasadena, California. Her father, John McWilliams, had a successful career in land management and real estate. Her mother, Julia Weston McWilliams, came from an established New England manufacturing family and ran her household with the assistance of a cook and a maid. Child would later admit that as a young girl, she had "zero interest in the stove" and "just didn't see the point" in cooking.

Julia followed in her mother's footsteps by enrolling at Smith College, an elite women's college in Northampton, Massachusetts. She graduated in 1934 and began to pursue a career as an advertising copywriter. In 1942, she took a job with the United States Information Service to do her part for the war effort. She later transferred to the Office of Strategic Services (the predecessor to the Central Intelligence Agency). While posted in Ceylon (now Sri Lanka), she met Paul Child, a sophisticated artist and poet with a black belt in judo and a taste for fine food.

Julia and Paul were married in 1946. Three years later, Paul was posted to the United States Information Service in Paris. Practically from the first bite, Julia was entranced with classic French cuisine. Determined to master French cooking, she enrolled at Le Cordon Bleu, the prestigious school that modestly claims to be "the guardian of French culinary technique."

Shortly after graduating in 1951, Child cofounded L'Ecole des Trois Gourmandes with Simone Beck and Louisette Bertholle. In addition to the cooking school, she joined their effort to create a French cookbook for American home cooks.

David Lyon

By the time *Mastering the Art of French Cooking, Volume One* was finally published in 1961, the Childs had returned to the United States. They settled into a house at 103 Irving Street in Cambridge in a neighborhood peppered with Harvard faculty. The roomy three-story gabled house behind a picket fence would be Julia's home for the next forty years. One of the first projects the couple tackled was to redesign the kitchen.

That kitchen—with all Child's carefully organized pots and pans and cooking utensils—is now one of the most popular exhibits at the Smithsonian's National Museum of American History in Washington, DC. The house is not open to the public, but food lovers still make a pilgrimage to view the exterior from the sidewalk. From the house, it's a short walk to Savenor's Butcher Shop and Market on Kirkland Street. It's impossible to miss. Child scrawled her signature "Bon Appétit" in wet cement at the door. Opened in 1939 as a self-described gourmet butcher shop and high-end grocer, Savenor's became Child's go-to purveyor for breast of veal, leg of lamb, and plain old hamburger. In fact, Savenor's provided all the meats for *The French Chef*, Child's groundbreaking show on WGBH.

In response to viewer enthusiasm for Child's now-legendary omelet demonstration, *The French Chef* debuted on February 11, 1963. The original series ran for 199 episodes between 1963 and 1966. By the time Child received her first of three Prime Time Emmys in 1966, her show was destination viewing on more than a hundred educational television stations across the country. That same year, Child appeared on the cover of *Time* magazine, which anointed her "Our Lady of the Ladle."

In many ways, Child was in the right place at the right time. Americans had become entranced with the French flair—and food—of the Kennedy White House.

Meanwhile, WGBH was looking to move away from its rather dry academic programming in the hopes of expanding its audience. Station managers could not have found a more engaging personality than Julia Child, the first public television celebrity.

Americans had not simply fallen in love with quiche Lorraine, boeuf bourguignon, and chocolate soufflés. They responded to Child's quirky personality and piping voice. Whether roasting bones for stock or frenching a rack of lamb, she tackled the task with joy and determination. As longtime *Boston Globe* food editor Sheryl Julian noted, Child "brought to television a lifetime of party-going, merriment, and far-flung adventures."

At more than six feet tall and a stickler for following recipes, Child might have been an intimidating force. Instead, she was encouraging and unconcerned with cooking mishaps. In the era before open floor plans put the cook on display, she told viewers, "Remember, you are alone in the kitchen and no one can see you."

Julia Child went on to publish a shelfful of books, including the posthumous *My Life in France*, with her grandnephew Alex Prud'homme. She also hosted ten different television series, often with other master chefs.

Child's accolades came from all corners. In a 1978 *Saturday Night Live* skit, Dan Aykroyd famously portrayed Child trying to stanch the bleeding from a self-inflicted knife wound. It was a sure sign that she had arrived as a cultural icon. On a more serious note, Child was the first woman inducted into the Hall of Fame of the Culinary Institute of America. Both the United States and French governments awarded her their highest honors. Harvard University was one of more than ten universities to grant her an honorary doctorate, calling Child "a Harvard friend and neighbor who has filled the air with common sense and uncommon scents."

Child dined out often in local restaurants. She was committed to encouraging chefs, especially women, and to advancing the culinary profession. She often frequented Harvest restaurant, which opened in Harvard Square in Cambridge in 1975 and remains a favorite neighborhood haunt.

On the national level, Child joined with winemakers Robert Mondavi and Richard Graff to found the American Institute of Wine & Food in 1981. Their goal was nothing less than to "advance the understanding, appreciation and quality of wine and food." In 1995, Child established her namesake Julia Child Foundation for Gastronomy and the Culinary Arts.

After Paul Child died in 1994, Julia continued to live in their Irving Street home until she moved to Santa Barbara, California, in 2001. Julia Child died on August 13, 2004. Each year, her foundation presents an award to an individual or team who has followed in Child's footsteps by making "a profound and significant difference in the way America cooks, eats and drinks."

ISABELLA STEWART GARDNER'S MUSEUM
Isabella Stewart Gardner Museum, 25 Evans Way, Boston;
617-566-1401; gardnermuseum.org; open year-round;
admission charged

Transplanted New Yorker Isabella Stewart Gardner embraced Boston with a passion. She established herself as a hostess with a great guest list, attended concerts of the Boston Symphony Orchestra, sat in on readings at Harvard, watched the university's football and hockey games, and rooted, of course, for the Boston Red Sox.

She was such a passionate Red Sox fan that she arrived at Symphony Hall wearing a headband emblazoned "Oh, You Red Sox" to celebrate the team's 1912 World Series victory. Reporting on the incident, a gossip magazine of the day declared that it "looks as if the woman had gone crazy." That may be an overstatement, but Gardner was definitely unconventional. Despite reports to the contrary, she never walked lions on a leash through the Back Bay. But she didn't hesitate to follow her own instincts and pursue her own passions. She collected art with a seriousness unprecedented for women of her era, assembled one of the most outstanding private art

David Lyon

collections in the country, and then built a stunning, intimate museum to display her treasures.

Isabella Stewart was born into the wealthy family of David Stewart and Adelia Smith Stewart on April 14, 1840. She attended private schools in New York and Paris and was introduced to her future husband by a Paris classmate. John L. Gardner came from an equally well-off Boston family. When the couple married in April 1860, Isabella's father made sure that they got off to a good start by giving them an elegant mansion in the newly fashionable Back Bay as a wedding gift.

Like many members of their social class, the Gardners frequently traveled abroad. They took their first big trip in 1867, only two years after the death of their only child. As hoped, the journey through Scandinavia, Russia, Vienna, and Paris did help Isabella to recover from her grief. It also ignited her passion for fine and decorative arts. The couple began to fill their home with art and artifacts that they collected on their travels through Europe, Asia, and the Middle East.

Isabella became even more resolute in building an art collection when her father died in 1891 and left her an estate worth almost $2 million (about $50 million in today's money). She didn't waste much time in making her first major purchase the next year. She outbid both the Louvre and the National Gallery in London for *The Concert*, by seventeenth-century Dutch painter Johannes Vermeer. Two years later, Bernard Berenson assisted in the purchase of *The Story of Lucretia* by Sandro Botticelli. It was the first painting by the early Renaissance Italian painter to enter an American collection. Harvard-educated Berenson would become one of Gardner's most trusted advisors and admirers. She is "the one and only real potentate I have ever known," he once said. "She lives at a rate of intensity and with a reality that makes other lives seem pale, thin and shadowy."

In 1896, the Gardners made two major acquisitions. Titian's *The Rape of Europa*, painted in Venice in the 1560s, is considered one of the finest Renaissance paintings in America. The purchase of Rembrandt's 1629 *Self-Portrait, Age 23* marked a turning point for Isabella. It was the first painting that she bought with the intent of creating a museum.

"Years ago I decided that the greatest need in our Country was Art," Isabella recalled near the end of her life. "We were a very young country and had very few opportunities of seeing beautiful things, works of art. . . . So, I determined to make it my life's work if I could."

John Gardner died in December 1898, but Isabella was undeterred. That same year, she made a gesture of faith in the newly filled swamplands of the Fenway by purchasing land for her museum. Of all the places that the Gardners had visited, Isabella was most fond of Venice and decided to model her museum on a fifteenth-century Venetian palazzo. She engaged architect Willard T. Sears to help her achieve her vision. When construction began in 1899, Gardner visited the site practically every day and oversaw every detail.

When Fenway Court, as Gardner called it, was completed in late 1901, it boasted a glass-roofed central courtyard, three floors of galleries opening onto the courtyard, and fourth-floor living quarters. It took her another year to install her collections. It's hardly surprising that it was such a task: She had to place nearly 2,500 works of art, including paintings, sculptures, drawings, rare books and manuscripts, Japanese screens, and jewelry.

The objects in Gardner's collection span the globe and represent thirty centuries of creativity. She rejected traditional curatorial placements by chronology, subject, or geography, relying instead on her own instincts to create groupings that would "fire the imagination." Visitors will encounter, for example, a painting of the Madonna and Child by Botticelli hanging above an Islamic urn that sits next to a classical marble bust. The building itself, the collection, and its arrangement form a cohesive work of art—the vision of a woman with a singular eye.

A few lucky guests were invited to the unveiling of the museum on New Year's Night 1903. After a concert by members of the Boston Symphony Orchestra, they got their first glimpse of the courtyard, filled with flowering plants and illuminated by lanterns. In late February, the museum opened to the public. Admission was $1.

The courtyard at the heart of Fenway Court may be the first of its kind in an American museum. With its abundant greenery and a mix of architectural elements and sculptures that practically trace the evolution of Italian art, it is as much a delight today as it was in Gardner's time. Bostonians find it a welcome respite from the cold, gray days of winter and know that spring is on the way when long vines of orange nasturtiums spill down from the third-floor balconies.

Gardner lived in the fourth-floor apartment and treated the galleries as a particularly grand salon where she could welcome artists, writers, and musicians. Famous Australian operatic soprano Nellie Melba performed at Fenway Court, as did modern dance choreographer Ruth St. Denis. John Singer Sargent had a studio in one of the galleries. Several of his portraits of Gardner are in the collection, along with his haunting Spanish flamenco masterpiece, *El Jaleo.*

Isabella Stewart Gardner died on July 17, 1924. In her will she left an endowment so that Fenway Court could be maintained "for the education and enrichment of the public forever." She also left very specific instructions that her collection must remain intact and be displayed exactly as she left it.

Unfortunately, thieves had other ideas. On the night of March 18, 1990, two men dressed as police officers gained access to the museum and made off with thirteen works of art. The museum describes it as the "single largest property theft in the world." The case remains unsolved. Blank frames mark the spots where such masterpieces as Rembrandt's 1633 *Storm on the Sea of Galilee,* Vermeer's *The Concert,* and Édouard Manet's circa-1875 *Chez Tortoni* were placed by Gardner.

On a more positive note, a new wing opened in 2012 to relieve pressure on the original museum by taking over such visitor services as admissions, classrooms, a gift shop, and a café. The new Calderwood Hall performance space continues Gardner's tradition of musical concerts in the museum. The architect, Renzo Piano, acknowledged the primacy of Gardner's Italian palace in his own design, which he characterized as a "respectful nephew to the great aunt."

If visitors look closely, they will find ten actual images of Isabella Stewart Gardner in the museum, but her presence lingers in every room and over every object within her bold creation.

ROSE STANDISH NICHOLS'S BEACON HILL HOME

Nichols House Museum, 55 Mount Vernon Street, Boston; 617-227-6993; nicholshousemuseum.org; open mid-March through December; admission charged

Rose Standish Nichols was thirteen years old when her family moved into their Mount Vernon Street home in 1885. It was a prestigious address for prominent doctor Arthur Nichols, his social activist wife Elizabeth, and their three daughters. The 1804 townhouse had been designed by Charles Bulfinch, the architect largely responsible for developing Beacon Hill into Boston's most desirable neighborhood and creating its signature Federal-style architecture.

Born on January 11, 1872, Nichols would live in the Beacon Hill townhouse until her death on January 27, 1960. In her will she specified that her home should become a museum, offering visitors a chance to enter a fine Beacon Hill residence "without a letter of introduction." It's a rare opportunity to see what life was like behind the closed doors of one of Boston's most storied neighborhoods.

David Lyon

David Lyon

At a time when women had few options but to marry, Nichols became a model of a strong-minded independent woman. She invented a genteel career as a landscape designer, became a prominent social and political activist, and created Boston's own version of an artists' salon. Her museum, in fact, offers a peek at the lifestyle—and intensely lived life—of a Beacon Hill paradigm.

Nichols received an exceptionally well-rounded education in Boston's private schools. At Mrs. Shaw's School, founded by Pauline Agassiz Shaw, she studied history and the classics, mastered several languages, and became proficient in both needlework and woodworking. Tours of the Nichols House begin in the first-floor room that served as Dr. Nichols's office. Rose hand-carved the design on the four medieval-style chairs that surround a table. As a finishing touch, she stitched the needlepoint chair cushions.

Nichols also studied art, but her uncle, the sculptor Augustus Saint-Gaudens, directed her toward landscape design. It was a subject of great interest among the artists in the Cornish, New Hampshire, summer art colony that had coalesced around him. Nichols studied with architect and garden designer Charles A. Platt and embraced his formal Beaux-Arts style.

In 1892, Arthur Nichols purchased a property in Cornish, providing his daughter with her first opportunity to create a garden. The sunken walled garden with a distant view of Mount Ascutney was complete by 1895. Nichols was off to a good start. Garden writer Frances Duncan pronounced it "one of the most delightful gardens in the all artist-inhabited and garden-loving Cornish."

Because landscape design was just emerging as a profession, Nichols was left to devise her own curriculum to advance her skills. She continued to study fine art and architecture in Europe and in New York and studied horticulture at Harvard's Arnold Arboretum. She also became a "special student" at the Massachusetts Institute of Technology so that she could take an upper-level design course, where she "learned to apply architectural principles to the plans of gardens."

In 1904, Nichols received her first professional commission for a garden, at a Newport, Rhode Island, estate owned by one of her Beacon Hill neighbors. Over the course of a forty-year career, she designed more than seventy gardens, few of which survive. While many were located in New England, many others were created in Lake Forest, Illinois, where she worked closely with architects Howard Van Doren Shaw and David Adler, designers of numerous Lake Forest–area country estates.

Nichols traveled extensively and wrote three books on European garden design: *English Pleasure Gardens* (1902), *Spanish and Portuguese Gardens* (1924), and *Italian Gardens and Villas* (1928). She also contributed articles on gardening, interior design, and collecting antiques to *House Beautiful*, *Ladies' Home Journal*, and other magazines.

Nichols's Mount Vernon Street home—particularly the peach-colored parlor on the second floor—was her base for social activism. In 1896, she founded the Beacon Hill Reading Club so that women could meet to discuss the issues raised in new books of note. She was also famous for hosting Sunday afternoon teas where she encouraged "a friendly exchange of ideas in order to create a better understanding among people."

In 1912, Nichols invited Florence Kelley and Maud Wood Park, founders of the Boston Equal Suffrage Association for Good Government, to give a lecture in the

David Lyon

parlor. A firm believer in equal rights for women, Nichols became a member of the organization and also helped to found the Cornish Suffrage League.

Nichols was also instrumental in establishing the Massachusetts branch of the Women's Peace Party (WPP). Founded in 1915 and led by social reformer Jane Addams of Chicago, the WPP advocated for both peace and women's suffrage and gave women a strong voice in the pacifist movement. In fact, the WPP was one of the first peace organizations to advance the cause through public demonstrations. The WPP was incorporated into the larger Women's International League for Peace and Freedom and remains active today as the oldest women's peace organization in the country.

When Nichols inherited the Mount Vernon Street home in 1930, she focused much of her energy on collecting American decorative arts for her planned museum. The Nichols House Museum opened in 1961. Six decades later, it still reflects the taste and the spirit of its founder. Tours conclude in Rose's bedroom on the third floor, where she embroidered the draperies on her canopy bed and her sister Margaret built the bookcase in the corner.

A Sisterhood of Activists

Rose's younger sisters also made their mark. Marian Clarke Nichols (1874–1963) graduated magna cum laude from Radcliffe College and became an advocate for the rights of women and the working class. Among her many positions, she was secretary of the Women's Auxiliary of the Massachusetts Civil Service Reform Association for almost two decades. Shortly after women won the right to vote in 1920, she ran for the Massachusetts legislature. She did not win, but helped break the ground for women candidates for political office.

Margaret Homer Nichols-Shurcliff (1879–1959) was the only one of the three sisters to marry. She and her husband, landscape architect Arthur Shurcliff, had six children. Margaret developed a love for carpentry when she studied at Mrs. Shaw's School and eventually established a business with fellow carpenters Charlotte Ware and Theodora Jones. They called themselves "Pegleggers: Makers of Benches and Trestle Tables of Pine." Margaret also played a role in establishing the Massachusetts chapter of the American Civil Liberties Union. She was inspired by her father to take up the art of bell ringing and is credited with starting the tradition of bell ringing on Beacon Hill on Christmas Eve.

CATHERINE HAMMOND GIBSON'S VICTORIAN HOME

Gibson House Museum, 137 Beacon Street, Boston; 617-267-6338; thegibsonhouse.org; open year-round; admission charged

Comfortably ensconced on Beacon Hill as a widow in her fifties, Catherine Hammond Gibson became a pioneer by embracing the future of Boston. In 1859, she paid $3,696 to purchase a lot in the first block of the newly filled land in the Back Bay. It was a vote of confidence that the fetid tidal mudflats could be transformed into a stylish new residential neighborhood. Catherine's home was completed the following year and was one of the first to rise in the Back Bay.

Even as new land and new homes continued a blocks-long march toward the Fenway, Catherine remained one of the few women to own property in what became one of Boston's most architecturally distinctive neighborhoods. More than a century and a half later, Gibson House is one of only a few intact single-family residences in the Back Bay and captures the gracious lifestyle of the neighborhood's residents.

The Back Bay was designed for Bostonians like the Gibsons. Although they were not among the wealthiest, the upper-middle-class family boasted a fine pedigree of patriots of the Revolutionary War and successful merchants and traders. Catherine's father was a boot and shoe merchant and her mother was half-sister to William Dawes, who had ridden with Paul Revere to warn patriots of approaching British

troops. Born in 1804, Catherine married sugar trader John Gardiner Gibson in 1833. When her husband died only five years later, Catherine was left to raise their two sons, although only Charles, born in 1836, was living when she made her bold move to the Back Bay.

Architect Arthur Gilman, an admirer of French city planning, laid out the new land with arrow-straight avenues crossed at regular intervals with residential streets and specified plenty of open green space. Edward Clarke Cabot, who designed Catherine's Beacon Street home, channeled Gilman's sense of order in the design of the six-story redbrick and brownstone building with its symmetrical and modestly ornamented facade.

The home was a bit grand for Catherine and her son Charles. But Catherine envisioned a fuller family life and hoped that the fine property would be attractive to young women who might want to marry her cotton broker son. Catherine had a long wait until Charles married Rosamond Warren in 1871. Born in 1846, Rosamond burnished the family's pedigree by adding her lineage of China traders and physicians, including Dr. Joseph Warren, a hero of the Battle of Bunker Hill. Eventually, Charles and Rosamond added two daughters and a son to the family. In the 1880s, the six family members were attended by seven live-in servants.

Catherine must have been a pretty good mother-in-law. She moved from the master bedroom on the third floor to a smaller room on the fourth floor, across the hall from what became the nursery. Rosamond made the master bedroom her private

David Lyon

sanctuary and furnished it with the remarkable fifteen-piece faux bamboo-style bedroom set that she received as a wedding gift from her mother.

As was common at the time, Charles had a separate, but connecting, bedroom at the front of the house. The comfortably overstuffed library on the second floor was deemed the men's parlor. But overall, the home reflects the tastes and interests of the two matriarchs who shared it until Catherine's death in 1888.

Despite its restrained exterior, the Gibson House has a Victorian heart. The interior has all the hallmarks of Victorian taste: rich woodwork, fine finishes, lavish furnishings, and a profusion of artwork and decorative objects best accumulated by people who have servants to do the dusting. The formal dining room, with its arched carved doorway with etched glass panels and its elaborately carved black walnut fireplace surround, most bears Catherine's stamp.

Shortly after Catherine's death, Rosamond began to update the interior. The unusually large front entrance hall with a grand staircase was meant to make a good first impression on guests. It also best represents the merging of the tastes of the two mistresses of the house. The dark walnut woodwork and heavy furniture are original features, while Rosamond added the embossed and gilt wallpaper that would catch and reflect light. The family often entertained guests in the music room on the second floor. To brighten the room, she had the woodwork and some of the furniture painted white and added yellow-and-rose-colored vertically striped wallpaper.

Rosamond continued to live in the house after her husband's death in 1916. She taught voice and engaged in the sort of charitable activities favored by women of her social standing. She volunteered at Boston Lying-In Hospital, one of the earliest maternity hospitals in the country, and helped to found a charitable sewing circle called the "Maiden Aunts."

Shortly before Rosamond's death in 1934, her son Charles Hammond Gibson, Jr., moved back into his family home. Known to all as "Charlie," he led a colorful life as a writer, horticulturist, preservationist, and advocate for public parks. A gay man who styled himself a bon vivant, he turned his father's bedroom into a study where he could entertain close friends or settle at his desk to write.

Charlie had a fond attachment to the Victorian lifestyle of his youth. Realizing that his family home embodied a particularly seemly niche in Boston history, he founded the Gibson Society in 1936 with the aim of preserving the house. By the time he died in 1954, his action seemed all the more prescient. The neighborhood was in transition as descendants of its founding families moved to the suburbs and the stately Victorian row houses were divided into apartments or sold to universities and other institutions.

Three years after Charlie's death, the Gibson House Museum—filled with the family's prized possessions—opened to the public. It remains a time capsule of a vanished way of life and a testament to Catherine Hammond Gibson's determination to create a home that nurtured her family for three generations.

MARY BAKER EDDY'S CHRISTIAN SCIENCE CHURCH

Mary Baker Eddy Library, 210 Massachusetts Avenue, Boston; 617-450-7000; marybakereddylibrary.org; open year-round; admission charged for Mapparium

The Mother Church, 250 Massachusetts Avenue, Boston; 617-450-2000; christianscience.com; open year-round for services and free tours

Library of Congress

History records very few women who founded a major religious movement. New Englander Mary Baker Eddy, however, did just that by merging her religious faith and distrust of traditional medicine to form the Church of Christ, Scientist. From the outset, her belief in the power of faith to heal physical ailments attracted both converts and skeptics. But there is no denying that Mary Baker Eddy herself is a case study of a very determined self-made woman.

Her accomplishment is all the more remarkable given that Eddy lived in an era when women were barred from most professions and had to struggle to make their voices heard beyond their homes and families. Nothing in Eddy's early life suggests that she would triumph against all odds to emerge as an influential thinker of her day, famous as an author, speaker, and publisher.

Mary Baker was born on July 16, 1821, on a farm in Bow, New Hampshire. Mark and Abigail Baker raised their six children in the Congregational Church. Mary, the youngest, was often sick and unable to attend school. She satisfied her intellectual curiosity by reading and writing stories and poems at home.

Marriage was one of the few paths open to young women of Mary's generation, and she married building contractor George Washington Glover in 1843. She found, however, that marriage did not initially offer the financial security or domestic contentment she had expected. Glover, unfortunately, died the following year, three months before the birth of their son George, who would be Eddy's only child.

Her 1853 marriage to itinerant dentist Daniel Patterson lasted for twenty years, but the couple often lived separately.

Throughout that time, Eddy suffered from chronic illness and sought relief through a number of alternative treatments. She was most intrigued by the popular hypnotist and charismatic healer Phineas Quimby of Portland, Maine, who expounded on the influence of thought and spiritual belief to heal physical ailments. Quimby, however, died shortly before Eddy was left bedridden after a fall on an icy sidewalk. As was often her practice, she sought comfort in the Bible. Rather miraculously, she found herself suddenly well as she was reading a biblical account of healing. This sudden turn of fortune, she would later recall, was the moment when she discovered Christian Science.

Not that her full-fledged belief system came in a flash. Eddy spent nine years immersed in the study of scripture and the practice of spiritual healing and teaching before she published her foundational work, *Science and Health with Key to the Scriptures*, in 1875. The book laid out what she understood to be both the scientific and biblical foundation for spiritual regeneration and healing. Its central tenet that all matter was illusion shared much with the various forms of spiritualism popular during her time. But no spiritualists elaborated the simple tenet into a complete code of belief—a position she made very clear in Chapter IV.

Science and Health became a best-seller and made Eddy a wealthy and famous public figure. In 1877, she married one of her students, Asa Gilbert Eddy, and assumed the name by which she is still known around the world. He proved to be a supportive husband until his death in 1882.

Although Eddy attracted many adherents to Christian Science, traditional Christian sects were less receptive to her ideas. Taking matters into her own hands, she founded the First Church of Christ, Scientist in 1879 "to commemorate the word and works of our Master, which should reinstate primitive Christianity and its lost element of healing." Two years later, she launched the Massachusetts Metaphysical College, where she and others taught her system of healing for almost a decade and helped spread the reach of her church.

In 1894, Eddy built the first church building for her congregation in Boston's Back Bay. She called the modest little church "our prayer in stone." It became the nucleus of the current Christian Science World Headquarters, one of the most monumental public spaces in Boston. The original church is now the chapel behind the more grandiose basilica added in 1903–6. The basilica is the site of weekly worship services. The space reverberates with the sonorous swell of the largest Aeolian Skinner organ in the Western Hemisphere.

The complex acquired its orderly monumentality during a 1968–73 makeover by the legendary design firms of I. M. Pei & Partners and Cossutta & Ponte. By adding the world headquarters building and sculpting a limestone plaza to create a new

David Lyon

entrance on Massachusetts Avenue, they created a soaring and spacious complex. Its 700-foot-long reflecting pool is a popular spot for picnic lunches and evening strolls.

The adjacent building holds the Mary Baker Eddy Library, which documents the life and impact of Eddy and the influence of the Christian Science Church. The building also holds the Mapparium, one of Boston's hidden treasures. The three-story stained glass globe forever fixes the world with the political boundaries of 1935. Visitors literally penetrate the heart of the world on a thirty-foot walkway

David Lyon

while an audio narration outlines the events and issues of that time. Other exhibits highlight significant accomplishments and milestones in the ensuing decades.

A year before her death on December 3, 1910, Eddy established the *Christian Science Monitor* newspaper. She was eighty-six years old and accustomed to attacks on her unorthodox beliefs. She was a particular target of Joseph Pulitzer, the publisher of one of the era's most sensational newspapers, the *New York World*. Eddy determined to present the reading public with an alternative to the so-called yellow journalism of the day by publishing a newspaper with the express goal "to injure no man, but to bless all mankind."

Pulitzer's *New York World* went out of business in 1931. The *Christian Science Monitor* continues to publish and has, so far, won seven Pulitzer Prizes—prestigious awards established in 1917 according to provisions in Joseph Pulitzer's will.

Final Rest

Mary Baker Eddy selected Mount Auburn Cemetery in Cambridge as her final resting place. She told the Christian Science Board of Directors that she wanted "a beautiful burying lot" in one of the earliest garden cemeteries in the country. She is, in fact, buried at a lovely spot beside Halcyon Lake. Inspired by the ancient Tower of Winds in Athens, her memorial features a circular colonnade of eight marble columns, each fifteen feet high. Contrary to urban myth, there is no telephone in the mausoleum.

PHILLIS WHEATLEY'S HOUSE OF WORSHIP
Old South Meeting House, 310 Washington Street, Boston; 617-482-6439; revolutionaryspaces.org/osmh; open year-round; admission charged

Phillis Wheatley was about seven years old when she was given the name that would make history. Ripped from her home and family in West Africa, she was auctioned as a slave in Boston in 1761. The Wheatley family, who became her owners, called her Phillis, after the ship that brought her to America. Within a dozen years, she would become the first enslaved person—and only the third woman in colonial America—to publish a volume of poetry.

The young girl was a domestic servant to Susanna Wheatley, wife of well-connected merchant John Wheatley. Recognizing Phillis's curiosity and intelligence, Susanna and her children Nathaniel and Mary taught her to read and write. At the time, only about half of the women in the American colonies were literate. If enslaved people received any education at all, it was only to enable them to read the Bible. Phillis did read the Bible, but she also studied astronomy, ancient history, geography, Greek and Latin classics, British literature, and mythology. At the same time, she fulfilled her household duties.

Phillis was in her early teens when her first poem was published in 1767. Three years later, she wrote an elegy for the well-known English evangelical minister George Whitefield, who had died while visiting Massachusetts. It was published in several American cities and in London, bringing the budding poet recognition on both sides of the Atlantic.

Despite the accolades, Phillis was unable to secure publication of her volume of poetry in America. *Poems on Various Subjects, Religious and Moral, by Phillis Wheatley, Negro Servant to Mr. John Wheatley of Boston* was published in London in 1773. The young woman's accomplishment was so extraordinary that John Wheatley and other influential Bostonians, including John Hancock, vouched for her in a preface. They noted that "the Poems specified in the following Page[s] were (as we verily believe) written by PHILLIS, a young Negro Girl, who was but a few Years since, brought an uncultivated Barbarian from *Africa*, and has ever since been, and now is, under the Disadvantage of serving as a Slave in a Family in this Town."

The inquisition conducted before they issued this imprimatur resonates through the ages. "Essentially, she was auditioning for the humanity of the entire African people" by proving herself to these Bostonians, scholar Henry Louis Gates, Jr., noted in a 2002 lecture. "With the publication of her book, Phillis Wheatley almost immediately became the most famous African on the face of the Earth, the Oprah Winfrey of her time," Gates added. She was, in fact, one of the best-known poets in America.

PHILLIS WHEATLEY, NEGRO SERVANT to Mr JOHN WHEATLEY, of BOSTON.

Published according to Act of Parliament, Sept.ʳ 1, 1773 by Arch.ᵈ Bell,
Bookseller Nᵒ. 8 near the Saracens Head Aldgate.

Despite her youth, she corresponded with noted scholars and political leaders in the United States and Great Britain.

The 1730 Old South Meeting House, where Wheatley worshiped, displays a bust of the poet along with a first edition of her book. Boston's third congregation, originally gathered in 1669, was perhaps the most socially aware of the city's churches and a hotbed of radical thought when Wheatley attended. By tradition, Wheatley and other free or enslaved Black people would have sat in the balcony, while White colonists enjoyed the comfort of box pews on the ground floor.

Wheatley was released from slavery in 1774 and married John Peters, a free Black man, four years later. The couple struggled financially and found it nearly impossible to rise out of poverty in the economic depression that followed the Revolution. Phillis worked at menial jobs while continuing to write poetry and carry on her correspondence. It is estimated that she wrote nearly 150 poems, but was unsuccessful in getting a second volume of her work published in the United States during her lifetime.

Phillis Wheatley died on December 5, 1784. Her second book was published two years later.

Writing in the *New Yorker* in 2020, Elizabeth Winkler described Phillis Wheatley as "the mother of the African American literary tradition." Abolitionists often pointed to her accomplishments in their quest to end slavery and confer dignity on all people. In her own writings, Wheatley was more subtle than strident in her opposition to slavery. The grudging acceptance of her lot displayed in early poems evolved as she drew ever closer to freedom due to her spreading reputation. The strong Christian faith that sustained her also seemed to rein in her outrage. Ultimately, her poems did rebuke purported Christians for failing to come to a moral reckoning with their acceptance of slavery. An ardent American patriot, she often expounded on the virtues of freedom, expressing a thinly veiled hope that freedom from Britain might also lead to freedom from bondage for all.

Although the poet was dismissed by some as a pious apologist, scholars and writers have taken a more nuanced view of her work and short life in recent years. Henry Louis Gates, Jr., perhaps best summarized her significance as a poet, a thinker, and as the first writer of African background to become an international figure in modern times. "If Phillis Wheatley stood for anything," Gates said, "it was the creed that culture was, could be, the equal possession of all humanity. It was a lesson that she was swift to teach, and that we have been slow to learn. But the learning has begun."

A Trio in Bronze

Phillis Wheatley is one of three women honored in the _Boston Women's Memorial_ sculpture created by Connecticut-based sculptor Meredith Bergmann. Installed on the Commonwealth Avenue Mall in 2003, it's a welcome, if long overdue, addition to the statues of notable men that punctuate this green strip through the Back Bay. In addition to Wheatley, the sculpture features Abigail Adams (see page 130) and noted abolitionist and suffragist Lucy Stone (1818–1893). Ahead of her time, Stone insisted on an equal marriage, wrote her own marriage vows, and retained her family surname.

Unlike their male counterparts along the mall, the women don't stand on pedestals aloof from viewers. Wheatley sits with her left elbow propped on her pedestal and her pensive face resting on her hand. Stone reclines and leans forward with pen in hand, as if working at an editorial desk. Adams leans against her pedestal with her arms crossed and one foot forward.

"It gives me great satisfaction knowing that my sculptures make a difference in people's lives," Bergmann has written. "Bostonians leave notes on the _Boston Women's Memorial_ and put sweaters on _Phillis Wheatley_ when it gets cold."

ELMA LEWIS'S BLACK CULTURAL LEGACY
Museum of the National Center of Afro-American Artists,
300 Walnut Street, Boston; 617-442-8614; ncaaa.org;
check website for post-renovation schedule; admission charged

Even as a young girl, Elma Lewis had a clear sense of purpose. Reflecting on her childhood during a 1997 interview for the Smithsonian Institution's Archives of American Art, she recalled, "I was never developed to a life of leisure. A life of pleasant work, yes, but work." Explaining further, she said, "You come into the world to make it a better place. . . . That's what you're here for, to make the world a better place."

Lewis found her "pleasant work" in celebrating and elevating Black culture as the wellspring for a myriad of forms of artistic expression. Her single-minded determination combined with her creative dynamism to make her Boston's doyenne of the rich cultural expressions of the entire African diaspora.

Clairmont and Edwardine Lewis, immigrants from Barbados, welcomed their daughter into the world on September 15, 1921. The couple were followers of the Black empowerment philosophy of activist Marcus Garvey and brought their children to meetings of the Universal Negro Improvement Association. Elma absorbed Garvey's lessons of racial pride and self-reliance at the same time that she began her lifelong commitment to artistic expression. "I always knew what I was going to do, all my life," she said. "I was going to do things—to act, to dance, make music."

Lewis attended Boston public schools while also studying voice, piano, ballet, and tap. She worked with local theater companies while studying drama, dance, and costuming at Emerson College. When she graduated in 1943, she faced the harsh reality that few opportunities existed for African American performers. Never one to mince words, Lewis recalled that the only roles open to Black actors at the time were as "mammies or slaves." As she noted, "That was not going to be suitable to my temperament."

The following year, Lewis earned a master's in education from Boston University and found work as a speech therapist. She also taught dance and drama at the Harriet Tubman House and at other community centers. Before long, she took it upon herself to create the vibrant Black cultural scene that Boston lacked. In 1950, she founded the Elma Lewis School of Fine Arts (ELSFA) on the first floor of an apartment building in Roxbury, with a piano studio in one bedroom, an art studio in another, and a dance studio in the combined living and dining rooms. From the 25 original students, ELSFA grew to 700 students and 100 teachers at its peak. Lewis herself taught ballet and insisted on high standards for faculty and students alike. Many of her students went on to the kind of successful professional careers that she had once dreamed of for herself.

In 1966, Lewis launched Playhouse in the Park in Franklin Park. The sweeping parkland was the final gem in Frederick Law Olmsted's Emerald Necklace of Boston parks. But it had fallen into disrepair before Lewis launched a campaign to once again make it a safe and welcoming respite from the city streets. From 1966 to 1978, the Playhouse presented free performances every night from July 4 through Labor Day. Audience members might hear Nigerian drummer Babatunde Olatunji perform or Arthur Fiedler conduct the Boston Pops Orchestra. Duke Ellington, Billy Taylor, and Odetta were among the national headliners who made their way to Roxbury to thrill the crowds and support Lewis's vision.

Still more remained to be done. In 1968, Lewis founded the National Center for Afro-American Artists (NCAAA). The cultural center would create synergy between teaching and performing—and more fully realize Lewis's mission to showcase talented African American artists and to celebrate the rich culture that nurtured

them. In addition to the school, the NCAAA boasted professional performing companies in dance, music, and theater that spread Lewis's message of artistic excellence
throughout Boston and around the world. Classes and performances came to a halt
after a 1986 fire, but the NCAAA has presented Langston Hughes's gospel-inspired
Black Nativity to appreciative audiences every year since 1970. Generations of Bostonians have viewed or appeared in this beloved holiday tradition.

Lewis didn't overlook the wealth of Black accomplishments in visual arts. She
founded the Museum of the National Center of Afro-American Artists in 1980 to
encourage contemporary artists and to put their work in historical context of a long
lineage of Black art. In addition to its holdings in African, Afro-Latin, Afro-Carib-
bean, and African American artists, the museum has a permanent exhibit of objects
from the burial chamber of Nubian king Aspelta, who ruled all of Egypt from 600 to
580 BC. As always, Lewis thought big, declaring that the museum "is where we, the
Blacks, are going to state our Black heritage and share our culture and the beauty of
our arts with all people, Black and white alike."

The Nubian exhibition is part of the unique partnership between the NCAAA
and the Museum of Fine Arts (MFA), Boston, which excavated the tomb in conjunc-
tion with Harvard University. As Boston's flagship institution, the MFA also helped
guide the growth of Lewis's fledgling institution. The collaboration has benefited

David Lyon

both museums. NCAAA museum director and curator Edmund Barry Gaither has curated a number of exhibitions at the MFA to introduce broad audiences to the work of Black artists. When it opened in 1970, *Afro-American Artists: New York and Boston* was one of the largest and most comprehensive surveys of the work of contemporary African American artists presented in an American museum up to that time.

Elma Lewis was no stranger to honors and awards. In 1976, she was elected to the American Academy of Arts and Sciences. The MacArthur Foundation included her in the first group of recipients of a "Genius Grant" in 1981, noting that her efforts had opened the eyes of other institutions and spurred them to "expand their perspectives and interests to include African-American culture." Ronald Reagan presented her with the Presidential Medal for the Arts in 1983.

Elma Lewis died on January 1, 2004, secure in her legacy and in what really matters. Several years earlier she had told an interviewer for the *Boston Globe*, "When I leave here, the body of my work will be all these wonderful people out there in the world, doing great things."

CORITA KENT'S GIANT WORK OF ART
Commercial Point, Victory Road, Boston

Corita Kent spent only the last decade and a half of her life in Boston, but she certainly left her mark. *Rainbow Swash*, her design for the surface of a 140-foot-tall natural gas storage tank in Dorchester, is the largest copyrighted artwork in the world. The bright stripes splashed on a white ground have also stood the test of time as an icon of Pop Art.

Say "Pop Art" and most people think of Andy Warhol's paintings of Campbell's soup cans and wild parties at the Factory, his New York City studio turned hip hangout. But in Los Angeles, Pop Art also found fertile ground in the most unlikely of places: the convent and classrooms of the nun Sister Mary Corita. Kent chose that as her religious name when she entered the Order of the Immaculate Heart of Mary fresh out of high school in 1936.

Born Frances Elizabeth Kent in Iowa on November 20, 1918, Kent moved to California at age five with her devout Roman Catholic family. She attended parochial schools, and, after taking vows, continued her education at Immaculate Heart College in Los Angeles, a forward-thinking liberal arts institution associated with her order. She completed her BA in 1941 and soon began teaching in a primary school in British Columbia.

Immaculate Heart College made Kent a member of the art department faculty in 1947, about the same time that she began a master's degree program at the University of Southern California. That's where she found her artistic voice, so to speak, when she was introduced to the screenprinting technique that she would employ for the rest of her life. In 1952, only a year after receiving her advanced degree, Kent was awarded first prize in the Los Angeles County print competition and at the California State Fair. She referenced both medieval religious art and German

Expressionism in her masterful print *The Lord Is with Thee*, now in the collection of the Los Angeles County Museum of Art.

Kent created her first Pop Art print in 1962 after seeing an exhibition of Warhol's soup cans at a gallery in Los Angeles. She would later recall that "coming home you saw everything like Andy Warhol." Kent embraced Pop Art's appropriation of images from popular and consumer culture, but she added depth to her works by incorporating song lyrics, quotes from literature, and biblical verses. The rich mix enabled her to express both her faith and her increasing concern for issues of social justice.

By 1964, Kent was chair of the art department at Immaculate Heart and had begun to establish a national reputation as an artist. That same year, she created a fifty-foot banner for the Vatican Pavilion at the World's Fair in New York. In 1966, the *Los Angeles Times* named her one of their nine women of the year, noting that the "cloistered life puts her into daily and intense context with the realities and challenges of the human condition." Whatever limits religious life imposed, Kent nonetheless counted director Alfred Hitchcock, composer John Cage, architect Buckminster Fuller, and designers Charles and Ray Eames among her circle of acquaintances.

Newsweek magazine put Kent on the cover of the December 25, 1967, issue, under the banner "The Nun Going Modern." The accompanying article proclaimed

We Can Create Life Without War billboard, circa 1984. Image courtesy of the Corita Art Center, Los Angeles, http://corita.org

a "joyous revolution" among US nuns who were seeking greater involvement in the outside world and more direct ways to serve those most in need. Again, the author searched for the confluence of art and religion in Kent's life and ultimately concluded that "the nun, because her life is uniquely disciplined and largely stripped clean of irrelevance, has a rare advantage. Thus Corita finds it natural to bring her life to one sharp focus, to cut through the murky clouds of modern life like a single ray of sunlight."

Quoted in the article, Kent put it more succinctly: "The person who makes things is a sign of hope."

Kent soon proved that she did not need the structure of the religious order to flourish as an artist. In 1968, she received dispensation from her vows and left the Order of the Immaculate Heart of Mary that had been her home for more than thirty years. She settled in Boston in 1970 and was still a newcomer to the city when the Boston Gas Company commissioned her to create *Rainbow Swash* for one of their natural gas storage tanks a year later. Kent painted her design of stripes onto a seven-inch model that guided sign painters to reproduce the image on the 140-foot-tall tank. Other commissions included a "Love" stamp for the US Postal Service issued in 1985 and an antiwar billboard for Physicians for Social Responsibility in 1983. Kent considered the billboard, which boldly proclaimed "We can create life without war," to be a religious statement.

Corita Kent died on September 18, 1986, but the legacy of her artistic vision endures. Her works are in more than fifty museums, including the Metropolitan Museum of Art, the National Gallery of Art, the Whitney Museum of Art, and the Museum of Fine Arts, Boston. In a 2015 exhibition at the Harvard Art Museums, curators noted that "Kent is often seen as a curiosity or an anomaly in the pop art movement." But, they argued, "she is an innovative contemporary of Andy Warhol, Edward Ruscha, Roy Lichtenstein, Jim Dine, Robert Indiana, and other pop art icons."

It's an easy bet that none of those male artists produced a work of art that matches Kent's gas tank in scale—or in its unbridled exuberance. Kent found her place in her adopted city and left behind a grace note of joy. *Rainbow Swash* is a welcome sight to drivers who approach the city on the traffic-clogged Southeast Expressway. When the failing tank was scrapped in the 1990s, Bostonians were so distraught that Boston Gas ordered Kent's design painted on a replacement tank. To this day, the image remains a favorite city landmark as well as a testament to the artist and activist whose faith never wavered.

JACQUELINE KENNEDY'S LEGACY

John F. Kennedy Presidential Library and Museum, Columbia Point, Boston; 617-514-1600; jfklibrary.org; open year-round; admission charged

Jacqueline Lee Bouvier Kennedy Onassis: her name alone tells a story of a remarkable life. But for purposes of this book, she will remain Jacqueline Kennedy. She may have made her greatest mark in Washington, DC, where she was first lady for almost three years, and then later in Manhattan, where she was a book editor and historic preservationist for almost two decades. But New England also played a role in Kennedy's life, especially during her formative years.

Jacqueline Lee Bouvier was born in Southampton, New York, on July 28, 1929, to Janet Norton Lee Bouvier and stockbroker John Vernou Bouvier III. She lived and attended private schools in Manhattan and spent summers with the Bouvier family in East Hampton on the south fork of Long Island.

Kennedy's center of gravity shifted after her parents divorced and her mother married stockbroker and lawyer Hugh D. Auchincloss II in 1942. Janet and her two daughters relocated to Auchincloss's home in McLean, Virginia, and would travel by train to spend the summers at Hammersmith Farm, his family estate in Newport, Rhode Island. The twenty-eight-room shingle-style mansion was built in 1887 on a hill overlooking Narragansett Bay. True to its name, the ninety-acre property was home to Rhode Island Red hens, dogs, cows, and horses. The gentleman's farm also figured in Newport society. Kennedy began her debutante season with a tea dance at Hammersmith in the summer of 1947.

John Fitzgerald Kennedy and Jacqueline Lee Bouvier chose Newport as the site of their marriage on September 12, 1953. The ceremony was held at St. Mary's Church (123 William Street), an 1847 Gothic Revival–style building known for its forty-two stained glass windows created by the Tyrol Art Glass Company in Austria. The wedding reception for 1,200 guests was held at Hammersmith Farm. Photos of the day capture the young couple standing on the lawn as the bride's long veil floats in the breeze.

John F. Kennedy is most closely associated with his family's estate in Hyannis Port, Massachusetts, but during his abbreviated presidency, Hammersmith served as a more private getaway. Located at 225 Harrison Avenue, the property is not open to the public, although visitors often drive past for a fleeting glimpse of the Camelot years.

Within a month of John F. Kennedy's assassination on November 22, 1963, Jacqueline Kennedy and other advisors began plans for the presidential library that would secure the legacy of the thirty-fifth president and encourage others to follow his path into public service. In 1964, his widow laid out her goals for the library, writing that "it will be, we hope, not only a memorial to President Kennedy but a living center of study of the times in which he lived, which will inspire the ideals of democracy and freedom in young people from all over the world."

Kennedy was actively involved in the selection of architect I. M. Pei to design the building on a ten-acre site on Columbia Point overlooking the Atlantic Ocean. The ground-breaking ceremony was held on June 12, 1977, and the library was dedicated on October 20, 1979. Pei created an elegant geometric building of black and white masses planted on gray slate. It seems to jut into the wind over the harbor like a clipper ship's sails. Following Pei's careful progression of interior spaces, visitors end

David Lyon

their journey in a light-filled glass pavilion looking out at the sea and the sky. At the dedication, Pei spoke of the eloquence of the contemplative space.

"In the silence of that high, light-drenched space, the visitors will be alone with their thoughts," he said. "And in the reflective mood that the architecture seeks to engender, they may find themselves thinking of John F. Kennedy in a different way. In the skyline of his city, in the distant horizons toward which he led us, in the canopy of space into which he launched us, visitors may experience revived hope and promise for the future."

Jacqueline Kennedy remained closely involved in the library until her death on May 19, 1994. She helped establish an oral history project to capture the memories of members of the administration and others close to the president. It was the first such large-scale effort in a presidential library. She was also instrumental in acquiring the papers of author Ernest Hemingway in 1968. She saw the library assuming the role of a lens on American civilization, reflecting the cultural and social achievements of the administration as well as its impact on politics and governance.

No chronicle of the Kennedy presidency would be complete without recognizing the contributions of one of the youngest first ladies in the history of the United States. Whether working on the 1960 presidential campaign or greeting foreign heads of state or artists at the White House, Jacqueline Kennedy's presence permeates the museum exhibits.

A compact gallery contains photographs chronicling Jacqueline Kennedy's life from childhood to first lady. Soon after moving to 1600 Pennsylvania Avenue, she launched an ambitious project to restore the state rooms of the White House to reflect the historic importance of the building itself and to underscore the dignity of the office of President of the United States. She gathered experts in historic preservation and the decorative arts to help guide the undertaking. She also created the White House Historical Association and oversaw the publication of an official guide to the White House. Funds from the sale of the book helped to support the $2 million restoration.

The project moved quickly and Kennedy was able to unveil the gracious new rooms on the CBS prime-time special *A Tour of the White House with Mrs. John F. Kennedy* on February 14, 1962. More than eighty million viewers saw Kennedy serve as gracious hostess to correspondent Charles Collingwood. The first televised tour of the White House now plays continuously next to a display case with a replica of the red dress that Kennedy wore and a copy of the first-ever official White House guidebook. It encapsulates Jacqueline Kennedy's passionate commitment to historic preservation. She would remain an ardent champion of that cause for the rest of her life.

NINA FLETCHER LITTLE'S FOLK ART–FILLED SUMMER HOME

Cogswell's Grant, 60 Spring Street, Essex; 978-768-3632; historicnewengland.org; open June through mid-October; admission charged

By all accounts, Nina Fletcher Little had a discerning eye and ironclad confidence in her own taste. Although conventional wisdom held that colonial-era homes were either painted white or clad in silvery weathered shingles, she chose a sunny orange-yellow (which she called persimmon) for the exterior of the 1728 farmhouse that she and her husband, Bertram K. Little, purchased as a summer home in 1937. They named it Cogswell's Grant after John Cogswell, recipient of the original 1636 grant for the prime parcel of land that he transformed into a tidewater farm overlooking salt marshes and the winding Essex River.

The Littles began collecting antiques soon after they married in 1925. They frequented country auctions and modest shops as they sought out quotidian craftsman-made pieces, especially for their rustic summer cottage getaway in Hudson, Massachusetts. By the time they upgraded their summer digs to Cogswell's Grant, they needed more space for their three children and for their swiftly expanding collections. What may have begun as a pleasant pastime or an exercise in frugality had become a curiosity-driven passion that would engage the couple for the rest of their lives.

By Abbot Lowell Cummings, courtesy of Historic New England

David Lyon

Bert pursued a career in publishing and later served from 1947 to 1970 as corresponding secretary for the Society for the Preservation of New England Antiquities (SPNEA), now Historic New England. Nina, meanwhile, brought a similar professional dedication to their collecting. "Although Nina Little always shared her research and collecting interests with her husband, she was unquestionably the moving force behind their collecting," fellow preservationist Jane Nylander wrote in a 1993 obituary of Nina for the American Antiquarian Society.

The Littles decided to fill Cogswell's Grant with furniture and decorative objects contemporaneous with the house and preferably from Essex County. When word spread that the Littles were interested in "old stuff," their neighbors were more than happy to open their barns and attics. The couple especially relished the ingenuity and imagination of the untrained artisans who brought a sense of character and creativity to everyday objects. Bucking the fine arts establishment, which found little value in early American folk arts, the Littles embarked on what Nina called "a hitherto unexplored territory of collecting and research." The time was ripe to rescue pieces long out of fashion that heirs were nonetheless reluctant to consign to the trash.

Nina's interest went well beyond the weathervane or painted chest itself—or even the thrill of the hunt. She wanted to know as much as possible about who had made each object and who had commissioned it or owned it. "Those who collect knowledge along with their teapots will seldom be downhearted and will never be bored," she once wrote.

David Lyon

By her own admission, Nina relished "being the old detective." Largely self-taught, she brought a high level of order and discipline to her research. She and Bert left no source unmined, gleaning information about objects, their makers, and their owners from historical societies, town archives, genealogical societies, probate courts, old cemeteries, and—when possible—living descendants.

Nina kept a small office at Cogswell's Grant with a manual typewriter, rotary telephone, several loose-leaf binders, and shelves covered with more carved birds than reference books. Her command center, however, occupied two rooms in the couple's year-round home in Brookline, the town where Nina had been born in 1903. She assembled an extensive reference library and surrounded herself with card files, notebooks, and photographs to bring order to the expanding collections and to focus the corresponding research.

In a 1976 interview with Richard Nylander, then-curator of collections at SPNEA, Nina noted, "I feel it isn't just owning the pieces to put in one's rooms, but one has a responsibility to preserve properly the early history and the historical and family connections of the pieces one has."

As the author of more than 150 articles, books, and exhibition catalogs, Nina helped legitimize and advance the study of American folk art and became a much sought-after expert. She took particular interest in uncovering the identities of previously anonymous folk art portraitists. In 1947, she curated an exhibition of the work of eighteenth-century painter Winthrop Chandler at the Worcester Art Museum. It was one of the first times that a fine arts museum recognized the contributions of a folk painter. The field of folk arts had gained considerable respect by 1976 when

David Lyon

Nina and Bert worked jointly on the exhibition *New England Provincial Painters* as part of the celebration of the American Bicentennial at the Museum of Fine Arts, Boston.

In the 1950s, Nina helped with the design of the Abby Aldrich Rockefeller Folk Art Museum at Colonial Williamsburg, Virginia, and wrote the first catalog of the collection. It was the first museum in the country with a sole focus on this American artistic tradition. In that same decade, Nina helped develop the furnishing plan for the 1796 Salem Towne House at Old Sturbridge Village in Sturbridge, Massachusetts. Ever the researcher, she studied probate inventories and other documents in order to accurately portray the way of life of a successful businessman, farmer, and community leader. Such research is now common practice at historic sites.

For their own part, the Littles filled Cogswell's Grant with objects that delighted and fascinated them: painted furniture, unusual rocking chairs, hooked rugs, redware pottery, landscapes and seascapes, early painted portraits, decoys, and lots of boxes. In fact, one of Nina's books, *Neat & Tidy*, dealt exclusively with boxes. The couple preferred the term "country arts" rather than "folk arts" and never lost sight of the fact that the pieces in their collection were made to be used. So that's what they did.

Nina and Bert never treated their home as a museum, but it became one after their deaths, a few months apart in 1993. Now a property of Historic New England, Cogswell's Grant offers visitors an unusual opportunity to see a world-class folk art collection just as its owners arranged it and lived with it. Collectors make pilgrimages to the farmhouse, and they must itch to turn over the pieces (strictly forbidden) to search for Nina's famous jelly jar labels where she recorded all she could about each prized possession.

JUDITH SARGENT MURRAY'S HOME
Sargent House Museum, 49 Middle Street, Gloucester; 978-281-2432; sargenthouse.org; open Memorial Day through Columbus Day; admission charged

When Judith Sargent was born on May 1, 1751, Gloucester was one of New England's major shipbuilding ports and her father, Winthrop Sargent, was a wealthy and influential ship owner and merchant. Yet the benefits of her privileged family life only extended so far. In keeping with the times, Winthrop and his wife, Judith Saunders Sargent, did not believe that young girls destined for marriage, motherhood, and domestic life needed the same rigorous education afforded to boys.

So Judith was on her own. Denied an education equal to her Harvard-bound brother Winthrop, she took advantage of her family's extensive library to educate herself in history, philosophy, geography, and literature. She was only nine years old when she began to write poetry, and eventually she would become one of the country's earliest and most passionate voices for women's rights.

Following the path dictated to her by social convention, Judith married ship captain John Stevens in 1769, when she was just eighteen. They had no children but adopted two young girls, both family members who had been orphaned. The couple spent nearly a decade living with Stevens's parents before they were able to build their own home in 1782. Sited on a hill above Gloucester harbor, the Georgian-style structure featured large rooms, finely detailed woodwork, and a view of the harbor from the second floor. The home became a museum in 1919 and is filled with fine eighteenth-century furniture that reflects the family's standing in the community.

David Lyon

But appearances can be deceiving. The disruption in shipping caused by the American Revolution combined with unwise business decisions left John Stevens in serious financial difficulty. In fact, John and Judith all but barricaded themselves in the house for several months so that he could avoid debtors' prison. He finally escaped to the West Indies but died in 1786 before he could put his financial affairs in order.

Fortunately for Judith, her husband had signed the home over to her father. She didn't lose the roof over her head, but was forced to sell most of her belongings to help settle her deceased husband's debts. She would never forget how powerless she had been to manage her own affairs.

In 1788, Judith married the Reverend John Murray, an English preacher who had introduced the United States to the Universalist theology of salvation for all— as opposed to the Calvinist belief in an "elect" mysteriously chosen by God for salvation. Judith's father, Winthrop Sargent, had met Murray in 1774 and had become

David Lyon

an adherent of Universalism. By 1780, Sargent had constructed a small house of worship in Gloucester, which is considered the first Universalist meetinghouse in the United States.

Murray served pulpits in both Gloucester and Boston, but also traveled often as an itinerant preacher. He and Judith enjoyed a long correspondence before their marriage. Writing, in fact, is a thread that runs through Judith's life. By 1782, she was publishing poems and essays in periodicals of the day. In 1792, she began to write a column for *Massachusetts Magazine*, adopting the masculine persona of "The Gleaner" to encourage men to read her columns and seriously consider her ideas about expanding rights for women.

"Was I the father of a family," she wrote as The Gleaner, "I would give my daughters every accomplishment which I thought proper; and, to crown all, I would early accustom them to habits of industry and order that they should be enabled to procure for themselves the necessities of life, thus independence should be placed within their grasp."

Like Abigail Adams (see page 130), with whom she corresponded, Judith cast women's education in patriotic and practical terms, promoting the concept of American women as "mothers of the new republic." Simply put, she argued that the new democracy could not succeed without well-educated and well-informed citizens. Noting that it often fell to mothers to take the lead in educating their sons as well as their daughters, it was only logical that the women themselves should benefit from the best possible education.

Judith proved to be a prolific writer. She even had a play, *The Medium*, produced in Boston around the time that she and Murray moved to the city in the late 1790s. But she is best remembered for her seminal essay, "On the Equality of the Sexes," first published in 1790. She challenged the argument that men's intellect was superior to that of women, asking rhetorically, "Is it upon mature consideration that we adopt the idea, that nature is thus partial in her distributions? Is it indeed a fact, that she hath yielded to one-half of the human species so unquestionable a mental superiority?"

Having constructed her straw man argument, Judith responded with a resounding "no!" Women are limited, she argued, by lack of education and opportunity, not by any innate mental weakness. "Is it reasonable," she asked, "that a candidate for immortality, for the joys of heaven, an intelligent being, who is to spend an eternity contemplating the works of the Deity, should at present be so degraded, as to be allowed no other ideas, than those which are suggested by the mechanism of a pudding, or the sewing the seams of a garment?"

A good education would open many doors, Judith argued. She also advocated for a woman's right to work outside the home, to earn her own wages, and to manage her own finances. In fact, during both marriages, income from her writing helped keep her households afloat.

Judith and John Murray's daughter, Julia Maria, was born in 1791. Judith began educating Julia at home until she was old enough to enter an academy. She put her beliefs into action by helping her cousin, Judith Saunders, and Clementine Beach open the Ladies Academy in Dorchester to educate young girls in both the domestic arts and more scholarly subjects.

Judith also shepherded her husband's intellectual and religious legacy. After John Murray's stroke in 1809, the couple struggled financially but they did manage to publish two volumes of his letters and sermons. Following John's death in 1815, Judith completed and published his autobiography—a key work by one of the founding thinkers of American Universalism.

Shortly after the 1816 publication of Murray's autobiography, Judith joined her daughter Julia and her husband on his family plantation in Natchez, Mississippi. Judith Sargent Murray died in Natchez on June 9, 1820, far from her New England home and its intellectual ferment. But her ideas outlived her with a passion, inspiring generations of feminists, including Susan B. Anthony (see page 60), who was born the year Judith died.

THE MILL GIRLS OF LOWELL
Lowell National Historical Park; visitor center, 246 Market Street, Lowell; 978-970-5000; nps.gov/lowe; open year-round; admission charged for Boott Cotton Mills Museum

The opening of textile mills in Lowell in the 1820s signaled the beginning of the Industrial Revolution in the United States. The Proprietors of the Locks and Canals on the Merrimack River were the first to create a large-scale factory city where mills brought the entire manufacturing process—from bale to bolt—under one roof.

That ambitious venture also sparked a social revolution as young women left their family farms and small villages to seek employment in the mills. American industrialists were only too happy to adopt British textile technology, but they had good intentions—at least at first—to establish a more humane system of employment. English mills typically hired entire families, including young children, at low

David Lyon

David Lyon

wages. The Lowell proprietors reasoned instead that single women would be the perfect workforce for jobs that called for intelligence rather than great physical strength to operate complicated machinery. By deliberately employing young women, the Lowell system created the first class of working women in America. Soon, those women would also spark one of the country's first organized labor movements.

It's impossible to single out any one woman, but as a group, they helped to make the Lowell manufacturing experiment a success. By the mid-nineteenth century, Lowell was one of the country's largest manufacturing centers, with more than forty mill buildings stretching for a mile along the Merrimack River. Six miles of canals snaked through the city and earned Lowell the nickname "Venice of America."

The young women were paid in cash and lived in company-owned boardinghouses where they usually slept three or four to a room. A boardinghouse keeper spent much of her time preparing three hearty meals a day. She also closely supervised how the women spent their limited free time and maintained a strict 10:00 p.m. curfew. The women opened bank accounts and shopped for stylish clothes in local stores. But they paid a heavy price for what little independence they enjoyed. A factory bell organized their lives, summoning them to the mills where they worked for twelve to fourteen hours a day. They were granted a half day off on Saturday. Sunday was a full day of rest, although the women were expected to attend church services.

By the mid-twentieth century, all the Lowell mills had gone quiet. But the Lowell National Historical Park preserves some of the buildings, canals, and walkways that once made the city a hive of industry. The Boott Cotton Mills Museum occupies a

weave room with equipment that is still operable. Although it dates from the 1920s, the weave room gives a sense of the conditions that the early workers would have endured. The original textile mills were notoriously noisy, and park rangers hand out earplugs before visitors enter. Even when only a dozen of the eighty-eight looms on the floor are operating, the noise is so intense that it's possible to feel the air vibrate.

The national park also offers glimpses of the lives of those first women workers. The Mogan Cultural Center occupies a former boardinghouse and re-creates the early 1840s living environment. The kitchen, keeper's room, and fairly spacious dining room are on the first floor. The women's crowded sleeping quarters are above.

The women were expected to work for a few years before they left the mills to return home, get married, or seek other employment. They were encouraged to broaden their horizons through a variety of educational and cultural programs. Many women did eventually pursue other career paths open to them by becoming librarians, teachers, or nurses. One of the most well-documented of the mill girls,

Lucy Larcom, became a teacher, abolitionist, and writer. She's best known for her 1889 memoir, *A New England Girlhood.*

The written word figured prominently in the women's efforts at self-improvement. They formed literary clubs and for several years published their own literary magazine, *The Lowell Offering.* They also attended performances and lectures by speakers such as Ralph Waldo Emerson, Edgar Allan Poe, and Frederick Douglass. But for all their enthusiasm, the sad fact was that the women often found it almost impossible to muster the energy for a class or lecture after a long day on their feet in the mills.

One young woman neatly encapsulated the dilemma in her writings: "I well remember the chagrin I often felt when attending lectures, to find myself unable to keep awake. . . . I am sure few possessed a more ardent desire for knowledge than I did, but such was the effect of the long hour system, that my chief delight was, after the evening meal, to place my aching feet in an easy position, and read a novel."

When mill owners cut wages in 1834, many workers organized as the Factory Girls Association and organized a "turnout," or strike. As they rallied and circulated a petition, one of the owners declared that "a spirit of evil omen has prevailed." But, in fact, it was management that prevailed and also crushed a second strike two years later.

In 1844, the women organized again as the Lowell Female Labor Reform Association and often joined forces with the New England Workingmen's Association. With mill worker Sarah Bagley as president, the women employed much more sophisticated tactics in their quest to reduce the work day to a mere ten hours. They formed chapters in other mill towns in Massachusetts and New Hampshire. Although women were denied the right to vote, they successfully campaigned against a state representative who opposed their demands. They published pamphlets to shed light on the poor working conditions in the mills. Finally, they presented a petition to the Massachusetts legislature, signed by about 2,000 "peaceable, industrious and hardworking men and women of Lowell." Most of those signatories were, in fact, women. Some also testified before a legislative committee.

The New Hampshire legislature did become the first in the nation to pass a law limiting work days to ten hours, but the 1847 provision was not enforced. Legislative efforts failed in Massachusetts, but the pressure did force the textile mill owners to shorten the workday to eleven hours.

Beginning in the mid-nineteenth century, the population of the mills shifted as owners hired increasing numbers of immigrants who were desperate for work even under the poorest of conditions. The women organizers may not have achieved all their goals, but their initiative and determination earned them a place of honor in labor history.

According to the AFL-CIO, "the Lowell mill girls started something that transformed the country. No one told them how to do it. But they showed that working women didn't have to put up with injustice in the workplace. They got fed up, joined together, supported each other and fought for what they knew was right."

ABIGAIL ADAMS'S FAMILY HOMES

Adams National Historic Park; visitor center, 1250 Hancock Street, Quincy; 617-770-1175; nps.gov/adam; historic homes open mid-May through mid-November; admission charged

"Remember the Ladies," Abigail Adams famously wrote to her husband, John Adams, as he joined other patriot leaders to draft the Declaration of Independence. It goes without saying that the authors of America's founding document were all men. But with her impassioned challenge, Abigail secured her place in history as a proto-feminist decades before the term entered the American lexicon.

National Park Service

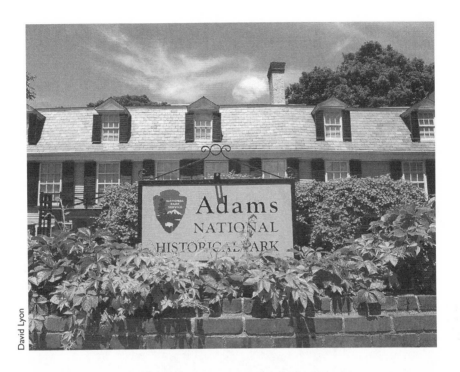

David Lyon

David Lyon

Abigail Smith was born in Weymouth, Massachusetts, on November 11, 1744, into a highly regarded family. Her father, William Smith, was a well-educated Congregational minister. Her mother, Elizabeth Quincy Smith, was the daughter of John Quincy, a colonel in the militia and a long-serving member of the Massachusetts Assembly.

Few young girls of the era received a formal education and, despite her family's standing in the community, Abigail was no exception. Fortunately, her father had an extensive library, and Abigail took her education into her own hands. She read widely, with particular interests in ancient history, theology, philosophy, government, and law—unwittingly preparing herself to become the most trusted advisor to the second president of the United States.

Abigail Smith and John Adams were married by her father on October 25, 1764, and moved into a small farmhouse in Braintree (now Quincy), next door to the equally modest farmhouse where John had been born. Those two houses and the larger home that the couple bought once they were well established constitute Adams National Historic Park. As expected, the site emphasizes the birthplaces and careers of two of the earliest US presidents. But the old adage that "behind every successful man, there is a strong woman" has perhaps never been more true. Although she operated largely behind the scenes, Abigail played a major role in her husband's political career and, by extension, in the birth of the new republic.

Abigail gave birth to five children (one of whom died in infancy) in the farmhouse and managed both her household and her children's education. She also took an active hand in overseeing the family's farm and finances, allowing John, a Harvard graduate, to concentrate on his law practice and travel as a circuit judge. Today's visitors find a comfortable family home with a painted clapboard exterior; extensive painting on the walls, floors, and woodwork; and homey touches such as hooked rugs on the floors.

The couple had begun corresponding during their two-year courtship and continued the practice throughout their marriage, eventually exchanging more than 1,100 letters. The sheer volume attests to the months and years they spent apart as John built his political career. When John was selected as a delegate to the Continental Congress in 1774, Abigail made a point of keeping him informed of the mounting political tensions in Boston. Her letters were first edited for publication by a grandson in 1848. They offer a firsthand look at a turning point in history and underscore Abigail's legacy of influence in the shaping of a new nation.

Abigail sometimes addressed her husband as "Dearest Friend" and didn't hesitate to make her opinions known. Unfortunately, her expansive view of equal rights and opportunity proved to be ahead of her era. When it came time to draft the Declaration of Independence, she wrote, "I wish most sincerely that there was not a slave in the province. It always appeared a most iniquitous scheme to me to fight ourselves for what we are daily robbing and plundering from those who have as good a right to freedom as we have."

In her most frequently quoted letter, she admonished John to "remember the Ladies, and be more generous and favorable to them than your ancestors. . . . Remember all Men would be tyrants if they could." She went on to caution darkly that if women's rights were ignored, "[we] will not hold ourselves bound by any laws in which we have no voice, or representation." Alas, seven generations would pass before American women won the right to vote.

Abigail also proved an astute social critic, realizing that denying the powerless an education was the most effective way of keeping them in their place. In 1778, she wrote that "you need not be told how much female education is neglected, nor how fashionable it has been to ridicule female learning." She suggested that the new country would be squandering an opportunity if it did not educate women. Ever pragmatic, she argued that knowledge would empower mothers to educate their children, shape their character, and groom new generations of leaders. Implicit in her argument was that those leaders would be men—she never underestimated the fragility of the male ego.

The correspondence flowed across the Atlantic Ocean when John left for Europe in 1778 on what turned out to be ten years of diplomatic service. Again Abigail kept things running at home until she finally joined John in 1784 for postings in France and England, where he became the first US minister to Great Britain. When they returned to Massachusetts in 1778, the couple moved into the Old House at Peacefield, a seventy-five-acre country estate about a mile from their original home.

They had barely settled in when John was elected as the nation's first vice president and served under George Washington from 1789 to 1797. Abigail called on her experience in European diplomacy to assist Martha Washington in planning and hosting state events. When John Adams succeeded Washington as president, he wrote to Abigail, who still spent considerable time in Massachusetts, "I never wanted your advice and assistance more in my life." She remained her husband's closest advisor and most ardent supporter. In November 1800, after the US capital was moved from Philadelphia, the Adamses became the first presidential couple to occupy the White House. They had barely unpacked before Adams lost his bid for reelection to his vice president, Thomas Jefferson.

The couple returned to the Old House at Peacefield, then still a working farm with orchards, in 1801. Placed among formal gardens, the decor of the comfortable manse would change with the times. The house would be home for four generations of their family of political leaders, diplomats, and scholars until 1927. Peacefield became a property of the National Park Service in 1946, followed by the two birthplaces in 1979.

Old habits die hard, and Abigail continued writing letters to political figures, including Thomas Jefferson, even as she devoted herself to her family. She took particular interest in her son John Quincy and the trajectory of his political career as diplomat, US senator, and secretary of state under president James Monroe. Abigail Adams died on October 28, 1818, and did not live to see the son whom she had named after her grandfather become the sixth president of the United States in 1825.

But history may have missed the mark. President Harry Truman once quipped that Abigail "would have been a better president than her husband."

Witness to History

On June 17, 1775, Abigail Adams and her seven-year-old son John Quincy walked about a half mile from their home to the top of Penn's Hill, where they had a clear view of the British bombardment of the American militia position on the Charlestown heights. Twelve miles to the north, cannon fire thundered before Redcoats began their ascent in the Battle of Bunker Hill. The British would ultimately prevail, but their Pyrrhic victory marked the beginning of the end of the royal occupation of Boston.

The full fury of battle was a frightful event. The next day she wrote to her husband that "the Battle began upon our intrenchments upon Bunkers Hill, a Saturday morning about 3 o'clock & has not ceased yet & tis now 3 o'clock Sabbath afternoon. . . . How many have fallen we know not. The constant roar of the cannon is so distressing that we can not eat, drink, or sleep. May we be supported and sustained in the dreadful conflict."

In 1896, the Society of the Daughters of the Revolution erected a stone cairn memorializing the spot at the corner of Viden Road and Franklin Street, Quincy. A small park surrounds the memorial.

MARY OLIVER'S NATURAL WORLD
Cape Cod National Seashore; 508-255-3421; nps.gov.caco

Beech Forest Trail, 36 Race Point Road, Provincetown; open year-round; free

Herring Cove Beach, Route 6, Provincetown; open year-round; admission charged in summer

Mary Oliver was one of the best-selling poets in the United States and the recipient of both a Pulitzer Prize and a National Book Award. But she didn't let the recognition go to her head. "I never advertised myself as a poet," she told interviewer Krista Tippett of the On Being Project in 2015.

David Lyon

Oliver spent more than forty years in Provincetown, the spiraling spit of land on the very tip of Cape Cod. "And there was that wonderful thing about the town," she continued. "And that is, I was taken as somebody who worked like anyone else." Her work, as she often described it, was "to pay attention," adding that "this is our endless and proper work."

Almost daily, Oliver immersed herself in the Outer Cape's rich mingling of spaces where land and sea conjoin to create an environment that is neither and both at the same time. She might follow the shoreline, skirt the edges of ponds and marshes, or plunge down a trail through the beechwood forest. Her work, as she put it, was to observe both the beauty and the unsentimental indifference of the natural world and to distill those observations into the written word. She always carried a notebook and was known to stash pencils in trees—just in case she suddenly needed a writing implement when inspiration struck.

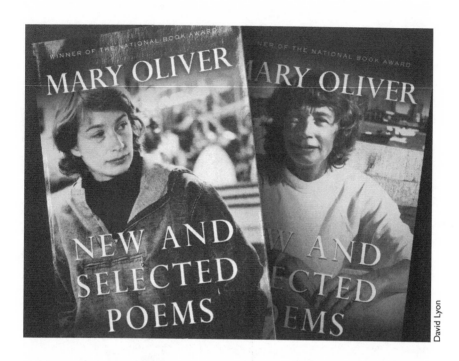

David Lyon

Beginning with *No Voyage and Other Poems* in 1963, Oliver published more than twenty volumes of poetry. They included *American Primitive*, which won the Pulitzer Prize in 1984, and *New and Selected Poems*, which won the National Book Award in 1992. She also published books about the art and craft of writing poetry as well as essay collections with prose as insightful, essential, and conversational as her verse. Although Oliver's work was often snubbed by critics, each new volume was welcomed by her many—mostly female—fans. She drew large crowds to public readings, becoming, as the *New York Times* noted in her obituary, "a reluctant, bookish rock star."

Oliver was born on September 10, 1935, and grew up in a troubled household in Maple Heights, Ohio. (Although she remained very private, in her 1986 book *Dream Work* she refers to abuse she suffered as a child.) She left home shortly after graduating from high school and studied at both Ohio State University and Vassar College, but never received a degree. Instead, she immersed herself in the life and works of Edna St. Vincent Millay (see page 174). Oliver spent several years at Millay's Steepletop estate in Austerlitz, New York, assisting Edna's sister Norma Millay Ellis in the organization the poet's papers.

On a return visit to Steepletop in the late 1950s, Oliver met photographer Molly Malone Cook, who would become her life partner. The couple settled in Provincetown in the 1960s. Cook opened a photography gallery, and later a bookstore. She also became Oliver's literary agent.

In her essay "Provincetown," Oliver describes their chosen home. "A tiny town as towns and cities are now, but to me it held a perfect sufficiency," she wrote. "Front Street and Back Street. Of course they had other names, but this is town talk. One traffic light, one doctor, one drugstore. A scattering of restaurants, saloons. And the boatyards."

It's easiest to imagine Provincetown as Oliver first saw it by visiting after the summer crowds have departed and the practical, hearty year-round residents have reclaimed their Front and Back Streets. But Oliver most often found her inspiration not in the town itself but in the wilder land and seascapes that surround it. She was, as fellow poet Maxine Kumin described her, an "indefatigable guide to the natural world." Oliver would walk the protected beaches along Provincetown's harbor or wander down the strand of slightly more unruly Herring Cove Beach at the west end of Provincetown, where town, forest, and sea all intersect.

Oliver was particularly drawn to the more hidden depths of the Province Lands forest. "The center of my landscape is a place called Beech Forest," she wrote in her essay "The Ponds." She didn't go so far as to reveal her private places, but the National Park Service's Beech Forest Trail traverses much of the same landscape that so transfixed her. The trail is an easy thirty-five-minute loop around a pair of ponds and through the forest of pitch pines and American beeches that colonized and stabilize the sand dunes. Boardwalks cross the swampiest parts of the trail. Otherwise, it's a sandy path, sometimes hard-packed and sometimes soft and loose. The woods are full of birds in the spring and fall. There are no signs, no verses calling attention to the rough lyric of the landscape. Walkers are, like Oliver before them, on their own.

Molly Malone Cook died in 2005, and Oliver celebrated their life together in the 2009 memoir *Our World*. Oliver's prose and Cook's photographs combine to create a portrait of the deep, mutually supportive life that many a couple would envy. Paying attention came naturally to her, Oliver writes. But watching Cook's intensity of vision brought a new level of depth to her own observation. "Attention without feeling, I began to learn, is only a report," Oliver wrote. "An openness—an empathy—was necessary if the attention was to matter."

About a decade after Cook's death, Oliver moved to Florida, where she died on January 17, 2019. "I don't know if I am heading toward heaven or that other, dark place," she had written earlier, "but I know that I have already lived in heaven for fifty years. Thank you, Provincetown."

MARIA MITCHELL'S EYE ON THE COSMOS
Maria Mitchell Association, Nantucket; 508-228-9198;
mariamitchell.org

Historic Mitchell House, 1 Vestal Street; open for tours mid-June
through August; admission charged

Vestal Street Observatory, 3 Vestal Street; following restoration, open
for tours mid-June through August; admission charged

Loines Observatory, 59 Milk Street; check website for Open Night
schedule; admission charged

Library of Congress

Thirty miles out to sea on the island of Nantucket, Maria Mitchell was sweeping the sky with a modest two-inch telescope when she spotted the blurry object that would change her life. The date was October 1, 1847, and she had discovered what became known as "Miss Mitchell's comet." As the first American to discover a comet, she soon became a star, so to speak, in the field of astronomy and a pioneer in opening careers in science for women.

Mitchell was born on Nantucket on August 1, 1818, the third of ten children of William and Lydia Mitchell, Quakers who believed in equal education for both girls and boys. Mitchell attended the local schools but she also studied astronomy, mathematics, surveying, and navigation with her father, an amateur astronomer. That proto-STEM education laid the foundation for her lifelong curiosity and fascination with the heavens.

In the mid-nineteenth century, Nantucket was the whaling capital of the world and even those who stayed ashore were often involved in the business. As Mitchell became known for her knowledge of the sky and her sharp analytic abilities, mariners sought her out to help them prepare for their yearslong whaling voyages. She taught sailors to use sextants for general celestial navigation, and by age fourteen was making solar and lunar observations to rate ship's chronometers so navigators could accurately determine their longitude. Her assistance gave Nantucket whalers a scientific advantage over many of their competitors around the globe.

Mitchell was only eighteen when she became the first librarian at the Nantucket Atheneum, established in 1834 as a membership library but now open to all. Her eyes, however, were as often pointed to the sky as to the books. She and her father studied the heavens from the observatory that he built on the roof of the Pacific Bank on Main Street, where he was a director and where the family had living quarters.

Mitchell's journal records her constant delight in the night sky. "The Aurora Borealis is always a pleasant companion," she wrote at one point, adding that "a meteor seems to come like a messenger from departed spirits." But father and daughter also turned their astronomical avocation to serious business, conducting observations for the U.S. Coast Survey, the first scientific agency in the country. (President Thomas Jefferson had established it in 1807 to survey the coasts and create nautical charts.)

After observing the comet in October 1847, Mitchell quickly published her discovery in the November 12 issue of Britain's Royal Astronomical Society's journal. Although other astronomers had also spotted the comet, Mitchell successfully made the case that she had been the first. In recognition of her accomplishment, she received a gold medal from the king of Denmark, Christian VIII, whose amateur astronomer predecessor had established the award for the discovery of new comets not visible to the naked eye.

As her reputation grew, Mitchell served as an official computer, calculating tables for the *American Nautical Almanac*. She also traveled throughout the United States and Europe to visit other observatories and meet with noted astronomers. In 1856, she became the first woman allowed into the Vatican observatory, which was located in a monastery that women were traditionally forbidden to enter.

To use modern parlance, Mitchell developed a habit of breaking glass ceilings. In 1848, she was the first woman elected to the American Academy of Arts and Sciences. (No other women received the recognition until 1943.) In 1850, Mitchell became the first female member of the American Association for the Advancement of Science. She later went on to serve as the second president of the Association for the Advancement of Women, which was founded in 1873. At the organization's fourth congress in 1876, she gave a passionate speech, "The Need for Women in Science," a theme that reverberated throughout her life.

Mitchell became the first female astronomy professor in the United States in 1865 when she accepted a position as one of the initial faculty members at Vassar College in Poughkeepsie, New York. Founder Matthew Vassar was committed to offering young women students an education every bit as good as that enjoyed by men and made a special effort to recruit Mitchell to the new college. The first building completed on campus was an observatory that held teaching space and living

MISS MARIA MITCHELL, PROFESSOR OF ASTRONOMY.

quarters for Mitchell and her widowed father. It boasted a twelve-inch telescope made by Henry Fitz, thought to be America's first professional telescope maker. At the time it was installed, only two observatories (including Harvard's) were equipped with larger instruments.

Mitchell and her students made good use of their top-notch facility. Mitchell took a special interest in the surfaces of Jupiter and Saturn, as well as their moons.

She studied comets, nebulae, and double stars and pioneered the daily photography of sunspots. At a time when few students of any gender did field research, Mitchell took her women students to Iowa and Colorado to observe eclipses. Their work was published in academic journals that typically only published men.

Mitchell's health was failing when she retired from Vassar in 1888. She died in Lynn, Massachusetts, on June 28, 1889. A month later, *Scientific American* noted that "she stands out clear and conspicuous, like an evening star in the heavens she loved so well to study."

In 1902, the Maria Mitchell Association was founded to carry on her commitment to nurturing understanding and love of the sciences. Based on Nantucket, the association is the steward of the 1790 home where Mitchell was born and opens it to the public during the summer. The association also operates the Vestal Street Observatory, built in 1908, and the Loines Observatory, with two domes built in 1968 and 2006. Astronomers and students follow in Mitchell's footsteps as they conduct research and offer the public a glimpse at the wonders of the night sky. The association also operates an aquarium and a natural science center, both named for Maria Mitchell.

Her name shoots through the heavens as well. "Miss Mitchell's comet" has long since disappeared, but an asteroid and a lunar crater also carry the name of the woman who once declared that "when we are chafed and fretted by small cares, a look at the stars will show us the littleness of our own interests."

CHRISTA MCAULIFFE'S SPACE MUSEUM
McAuliffe-Shepard Discovery Center, 2 Institute Drive, Concord; 603-271-7827; starhop.com; open year-round; admission charged

Every student should have a teacher like Christa McAuliffe, who had an infectious enthusiasm for learning. She was teaching history at Concord High School when she let her own dreams soar by completing the eleven-page application to become the first civilian in space.

President Ronald Reagan announced the Teacher in Space program in 1984 to build excitement and support for the Space Shuttle. Two decades earlier, Americans had been mesmerized by the United States' first manned missions into space and then on to the moon. But the seemingly more routine flights of the Space Shuttle lacked the sense of derring-do that had sparked America's pride and imagination. Seeking a way to connect with the public on a human level, Reagan reasoned that the first civilian in space should be "one of America's finest, a teacher."

About 11,000 teachers applied for the once-in-a-lifetime opportunity to make history. "We're not looking for Superman," NASA had explained. "We're looking for the person who can do the best job of describing his or her experiences on the Shuttle to the most people on earth."

Christa McAuliffe made a persuasive case to be that person. "As a woman," she wrote, "I have been envious of those men who could participate in the space program and who were encouraged to excel in the areas of math and science. I felt that women had indeed been left outside of one of the most exciting careers available."

The Teacher in Space program offered a different approach to the adventure of space. "I cannot join the space program and restart my life as an astronaut," McAuliffe continued, "but this opportunity to connect my abilities as an educator with my interests in history and space is a unique opportunity to fulfill my early fantasies. I watched the Space Age being born and I would like to participate."

On July 19, 1985, Vice President George H. W. Bush announced that she would be America's first civilian to travel in space. McAuliffe reported to the Johnson Space Center in Houston, Texas, in September to train with the six astronauts of the STS-51-L crew and backup teacher Barbara Morgan. McAuliffe also developed fifteen-minute lessons that would be broadcast from space to students watching on closed-circuit television. For "The Ultimate Field Trip," she planned to introduce her fellow crew members and explain how they were able to eat, sleep, and exercise in the microgravity environment of the Space Shuttle. To underscore the complexity of space

Courtesy of NASA

flight, she would also give students a glimpse of the 1,300 switches in the cockpit.

McAuliffe titled another lesson "Where We've Been, Where We're Going, Why." She intended to delve into the hybrid rocket-airplane flight of the Space Shuttle and talk more broadly about the allure of exploring space and the practical benefits of the technological advances that made space travel possible. The teacher was fully aware of the historic nature of her flight. She planned to emulate "the pioneer travelers of the Conestoga wagon days" by keeping a journal. "That's our new frontier out there," she said, "and it's everybody's business to know about space."

As NASA had hoped, the public was fascinated by America's first educator astronaut. McAuliffe charmed the viewers of *Good Morning America*, *CBS Morning News*, and *Today*. On *The Tonight Show*, she quipped to host Johnny Carson that "if you're offered a seat on a rocket ship, don't ask what seat. Just get on."

McAuliffe and crew members Michael J. Smith, Dick Scobee, Ronald McNair, Ellison Onizuka, Gregory Jarvis, and Judith Resnik climbed aboard the Space Shuttle *Challenger* at the Kennedy Space Center in Florida on January 28, 1986. They lifted off at 11:38 a.m. Then the unthinkable happened: seventy-three seconds into the flight, *Challenger* exploded, killing all seven members of the crew.

McAuliffe, who had been born on September 2, 1948, was thirty-seven years old and left behind her husband and two small children.

Christa McAuliffe was posthumously awarded the Congressional Space Medal of Honor in 2004. An asteroid, a crater on the moon, a crater on Venus, and numerous schools in the United States and abroad have been named for her. But the memorial that best honors her as a teacher and explorer is the McAuliffe-Shepard Discovery Center. It opened in 1990 as the Christa McAuliffe Planetarium, New Hampshire's official memorial to the educator astronaut. In 2001, the planetarium also became a memorial to New Hampshire native Alan B. Shepard, the first American to travel to space and one of only twelve people to set foot on the moon.

The space pioneer and the teacher he helped to inspire joined forces in 2009 in the re-envisioned McAuliffe-Shepard Discovery Center. The facility was greatly enlarged with the addition of a museum with interactive exhibits that unlock the worlds of astronomy, aviation, and earth and space science. It's a place where visitors of all ages can marvel at the wonders of space and the limitless possibilities of human imagination and ingenuity. The Discovery Center buzzes with schoolchildren on field trips or participating in summer STEM Camps.

McAuliffe, who was a great fan of field trips, would certainly approve. As she once famously said, "I touch the future, I teach."

GRACE METALIOUS'S DREAM HOME
Gilmanton Winery, 528 Meadow Pond Road, Gilmanton; 603-267-8251; gilmantonwinery.com; open year-round; tasting fee charged

In this less buttoned-down era, it's hard to imagine the uproar that greeted the publication of *Peyton Place* in 1956. Grace Metalious's debut novel exposed the shameful secrets below the surface of small-town New England life. Readers ate it up—buying 300,000 copies in hardcover and eight million in paper. Never mind that they often hid the book in drawers and kept it out of reach of their children. *Peyton Place* was, as *Vanity Fair*'s Michael Callahan reflected fifty years after its publication, "one of the best selling dirty books ever."

But *Peyton Place* was more than a best-selling novel. The mere fact that people still talk about it today proves its status as a cultural touchstone. Intentionally or

David Lyon

not, Metalious pushed the limits of what was acceptable subject matter in popular fiction, effectively giving her readers license to discuss such previously taboo subjects as child abuse, abortion, and incest. Equally important, as feminist scholars point out, *Peyton Place* delivered the powerful message to women that they should not be ashamed of their sexuality. In the process, Metalious all but created the publishing category of "blockbuster novel."

Born in Manchester, New Hampshire, to French-Canadian parents on September 8, 1924, Grace de Repentigny had enjoyed writing and making up stories since she was a young girl. She was still a teenager when she married George Metalious. The couple had three children and were struggling financially when Grace finally found a sympathetic editor for the book she originally called *The Tree and the Blossom*. Kathryn Messner, editor in chief and president of the small publishing firm Julian Messner, Inc., worked with Grace to shape the book and devise the title—*Peyton Place*—that would take on a life of its own as shorthand for scandal.

Predictably, reviews of *Peyton Place* were a mixed bag, but the unprecedented sales proved the old adage that all publicity is good publicity. The *Laconia Evening Citizen* pronounced the book "literary sewage," while the reviewer for the *New York World-Telegram* lamented, "Never before in my memory has a young mother published a book in language approximately that of a longshoreman on a bellicose binge."

The *New York Times Book Review* took a more balanced view, calling the book a "small town peep show," but also acknowledging Metalious for unmasking "the false fronts and bourgeois pretensions of allegedly respectable communities."

The Metalious family had lived in a number of small New Hampshire towns during the time when George was going to college and Grace was shaping her debut novel. When *Peyton Place* appeared, Grace and her husband and children had rather recently moved to Gilmanton, a rural community about twenty miles north of the state capital in Concord on the southern edge of the state's Lakes District. Most of their neighbors were shocked by Grace's airing of small-town dirty laundry, and perhaps fearful that outsiders might mistake their villages for the fictional Peyton Place. The backlash was bitter. George lost his job as teacher and principal at the Gilmanton Corner School, and the Metalious children were often bullied by their classmates.

Grace Metalious herself was utterly unapologetic about ruffling feathers. "To a tourist these towns look as peaceful as a postcard picture," she reportedly said. "But if you go beneath that picture, it's like turning over a rock with your foot—all kinds of strange things come out. Everybody who lives in town knows what's going on—there are no secrets—but they don't want outsiders to know."

Whatever criticism she endured over the book, *Peyton Place* made Grace a financial success. The family was able to move out of a dilapidated cottage with an unreliable well and into a handsome historic farmhouse that had been built in 1756, about thirty years after the town of Gilmanton was incorporated. After purchasing the property, she expanded the house, landscaped the grounds, and had an artesian well dug to solve the water problems once and for all.

The property is now the site of the Gilmanton Winery, established in 2011 by Marshall and Carol Bishop. The winery is open all year for tastings and purchases of its range of grape and fruit wines. One nook by the cash register is a bit of a shrine to Metalious, featuring an old manual typewriter, several photos, and copies of different editions of the author's works.

But the financial security didn't necessarily guarantee happiness for the Metalious family. Grace and George divorced in 1958, and the children split their time between their parents. Grace had a two-year marriage to disc jockey T. J. Martin, who encouraged her spendthrift ways and helped her down the road to financial failure. Grace and George did reunite for a while, but at the time of her death she was involved with British journalist John Rees.

Grace went on to write three more novels, *Return to Peyton Place* (1959), *The Tight White Collar* (1960), and *No Adam in Eden* (1963), though none achieved the buzz and sales of the original. For those who'd rather see the movie than read the book, 20th Century Fox released the film *Peyton Place* in 1957. It would go on to earn $11 million and be nominated for nine Academy Awards.

Grace Metalious died on February 25, 1964, and didn't live to see *Peyton Place* premiere on ABC's fall television lineup. The much-sanitized version of the novel is thought to be the first soap opera to appear in prime time. It helped launch the careers of young stars Mia Farrow and Ryan O'Neal and enjoyed a respectable five-year run of 524 episodes.

In many ways, Metalious was an unlikely literary star, which is perhaps why she continues to fascinate us. She preferred to dress in jeans and flannel shirts, drank to excess, and never became comfortable giving interviews. If asked a question that she didn't like, she could be downright prickly. But whatever her flaws, she was comfortable in her own skin.

Writing in the *New York Times* on the fiftieth anniversary of her death, Thomas Mallon observed, "Metalious's own experience of New England had included all kinds of want and unhappiness. She knew what she wanted to say about gossip and shame and small-town telephone party lines, and she could say it deftly."

David Lyon

GRANDMA MOSES'S FARM COUNTRY

Bennington Museum, 75 Main Street, Bennington; 802-447-1571;
benningtonmuseum.org; open April through December; admission
charged

Clara Sipprell, National Portrait Gallery

Perhaps the most acclaimed folk artist of the twentieth century, Anna Mary Robertson Moses spent much of her life in Eagle Bridge, New York, about fifteen miles from Bennington, Vermont. Better known around the world as "Grandma Moses," she is included in this book of New England women because the Bennington Museum is the steward of the largest public collection of her paintings. Moreover, Moses lived in Bennington in the early 1930s and painted rolling farmlands and country life with an abandon that ignored the state line between rural eastern New York and rural southwestern Vermont.

Moses became an inspiration to generations of late bloomers when she was "discovered" in her late seventies. Although she became an art world star seemingly overnight, Moses had an affinity for art from an early age. She was born into a farm family in Greenwich, New York, on September 7, 1860. Her father, Russell King Robertson, was also an amateur painter and sometimes brought home large sheets of blank newsprint as a treat for his children. Later in life, Moses fondly recalled her youthful attempts at drawing and painting on the paper, noting with the practicality of the farm wife she became that the paper "lasted longer than candy."

Moses studied at the one-room schoolhouse that has been relocated to the grounds of the Bennington Museum. She was only twelve when her education was cut short and she was hired to cook and clean for a well-off family. When she was twenty-seven, she married farmhand Thomas Salmon Moses.

The couple began their married life farming in Virginia's Shenandoah Valley. They returned to New York in 1905 and settled on a farm in Eagle Bridge. Moses raised five children (another five died in infancy) and never shied away from hard

David Lyon

work. She nevertheless found time for quilting and other needlework, and she squir-
reled away memories of country life that would eventually provide the extensive
subject matter for her work. Nothing was too small or too momentous to escape
her scrutiny, from mundane daily chores to the community-wide joy of a country
wedding.

Moses's husband died in 1927 and as farm work became too demanding, she
looked for other ways "to keep busy and out of mischief." She took up a needle and
thread to embroider scenes that she gave to friends and family. Eventually arthritis in
her hands made it too difficult to hold a needle—but she could grasp a paintbrush.
She returned to her childhood love of painting and began to draw from her rich store
of memories.

The images seemed to flow from her brush: chasing the Thanksgiving turkey,
hanging the wash, sledding down a hill, cutting a Christmas tree, sugaring off in
the spring. As a self-taught artist, Moses developed her own approach. She literally
worked from the top of the canvas downward, explaining, "First the sky, then the
mountains, then the hills, then the trees, then the houses, then the cattle and then
the people." Her work was instantly recognizable. Over the years, she made more
than 1,500 paintings.

Moses gave her early paintings away, sometimes sold them for a few dollars, and
displayed them at country fairs along with her preserves and baked goods. Her big

David Lyon

break came in 1938, when Louis D. Caldor, an art collector from New York City, saw a few of her paintings in the window of a local pharmacy. He bought them all, along with several others still at the farm. Caldor told the seventy-eight-year-old artist that he would make her famous. Moses was reportedly skeptical. She was, after all, unaware that the art world elite had taken notice of folk art. No less an arbiter of taste than the Museum of Modern Art (MoMA) in New York had elevated Self-Taught or Popular Art to one of the three "movements" of modern art—right up there with Cubism/Abstraction and Surrealism/Dada.

That enthusiasm perhaps explains why three of Moses's paintings appeared in the 1939 exhibition *Contemporary Unknown Painters* at MoMA—an exhibit that coincided with a forty-year retrospective of the work of Pablo Picasso. Moses's first solo gallery exhibition, *What a Farm Wife Painted*, was held the next year at the Galerie St. Etienne in Manhattan. Gallery owner Otto Kallir, who had fled Vienna after the 1938 Nazi invasion of Austria, typically represented top-of-the-line German Expressionist painters.

But Kallir threw himself into building Moses's art world fame through traveling exhibitions in the United States and abroad. Grandma Moses became a household name, certainly more familiar to most Americans than Paul Klee, Gustav Klimt, or any of her other gallery mates at St. Etienne. Moses created what she called her "old-timey" scenes to show people "how we used to live." Those images of simpler, reassuring times painted by a kindly grandmother struck a chord in postwar America. No one built home bomb shelters in Grandma Moses's world.

Moses was well aware of the power of her personality and published her autobiography, *My Life's History*, in 1952. The next year, she appeared on the cover of *Time* magazine. Edward R. Murrow interviewed her on his television show *See It Now* in

1955. The interview plays continuously in one corner of the Grandma Moses gallery at the Bennington Museum. As smoke wafts from the reporter's cigarette, Moses chats amiably about making soap and visiting the White House.

In addition to tracing her evolution as an artist, the museum fleshes out Moses's life with old photos. Media coverage captures the rise of Grandma Moses, the celebrity. The table where she worked and her well-used art supplies recall the more down-to-earth woman who is said to have declared, "If I hadn't started painting, I would have raised chickens."

Life magazine devoted its September 19, 1960, cover story to Grandma Moses's one hundredth birthday. She died a little over a year later, on December 13, 1961. In her autobiography, Anna Mary Robertson Moses expressed a sincere sense of fulfillment: "I look back on my life like a good day's work, it was done and I feel satisfied with it. I was happy and contented, I knew nothing better and made the best out of what life offered. And life is what we make it, always has been, always will be."

A Short Drive through Grandma Moses Country

The Eagle Bridge, New York, home where Grandma Moses lived most of her life as an artist is located just fifteen miles west of Bennington, Vermont, at 60 Grandma Moses Road, a turnoff from Route 67. A historical marker stands out front. The adjacent barn operates as Mt. Nebo Gallery and specializes in the illustrations of Grandma's great-grandson Will Moses. The road from Bennington is a scenic trip through a bucolic farming landscape surprisingly little altered from Anna Mary Robertson Moses's vision. It is also possible to visit the artist's modest grave in Maple Grove Cemetery, on the south side of Hoosick Falls, about five miles from her home.

ELECTRA HAVEMEYER WEBB'S MUSEUM
Shelburne Museum, 6000 Shelburne Road, Shelburne; 802-985-3346; shelburnemuseum.org; open mid-May through mid-October; admission charged

Electra Havemeyer was just a child when family friend Mary Cassatt captured her with her mother, Louisine Elder Havemeyer, in a charming pastel portrait. It probably seemed perfectly normal to the youngest child of sugar baron Henry O. Havemeyer. After all, she was living in a Manhattan mansion with interiors designed by Louis Comfort Tiffany and artist Samuel Colman. Paintings by Claude Monet, Édouard Manet, Paul Cézanne, Rembrandt, and El Greco covered the walls. The

David Lyon

Metropolitan Museum of Art, which received a major bequest following Louisine's death in 1929, describes the Havemeyer collection as "a legendary assemblage."

Electra was born on August 16, 1888, with her parents' passion for collecting in her genes. She was eighteen years old when she made her first significant purchase: a life-size cigar-store figure for which she paid $15. "I just had to have her," she recalled roughly a half century later in a 1957 Colonial Williamsburg lecture. Despite her mother's disdain for the folk carving, the purchase marked the beginning of Electra's lifelong collecting passion. She made it her mission to find and appreciate the beauty in everyday objects and to celebrate the purity and integrity of the work of untrained artisans. Other collectors and museums were slower to recognize the merit in simple American objects and folk arts, which gave Electra a head start in creating an unparalleled collection of what came to be known as Americana.

In 1910, Electra married James Watson Webb, a champion polo player and scion (on his mother's side) of the fabulously wealthy Vanderbilt family. The marriage cemented her status in the upper echelons of New York society, but it also introduced her to rural northern Vermont. Her husband's parents had created a massive estate and model farm on the shores of Lake Champlain, but Electra was drawn to the more down-to-earth values and material culture of the native Vermonters. Shortly after her marriage, she picked up the pace of her collecting and continued her acquisitive quest even as she raised five children and juggled three households.

Having plenty of property was actually a boon for the collector. Webb's Park Avenue apartment reflected the refined environment of her youth with its French Impressionist paintings and fine European and American furniture. But she filled her Long Island estate and her forty-room Colonial Revival home in Vermont with quilts, decoys, folk paintings, ships' figureheads, weathervanes, and all the other naive marvels that spoke to her as art.

Webb's private collections began to coalesce as a museum in the mid-1940s when the Vanderbilt family sought a new home for the magnificent collection of old carriages and sleighs that Electra's father-in-law had housed at their Lake Champlain property. At the Williamsburg lecture, Webb recalled her breakthrough. She proposed that she would keep the vehicles in a building on a piece of property in Shelburne. That, she said, "was the spark that lit the fire and I had my opening. And that was the start of the Shelburne Museum."

She founded the Shelburne Museum in 1947 and ensconced the carriage collection in a horseshoe-shaped barn that she had erected on the grounds in 1949. It was modeled after a dairy barn in Georgia, Vermont, some thirty miles north. The pairing helped establish the practice of displaying the folk objects in buildings with their own distinctive character.

Webb set about gathering old structures from New England and New York and reassembling them on the museum grounds. Each is a revelation. An 1832 Greek Revival home holds wildfowl decoys. An 1800 distillery-turned-barn displays quilts, hooked rugs, and samplers. A 1783 stagecoach inn houses cigar-store figures, ships' carvings, weathervanes, folk art paintings, and old trade signs. An 1835 Greek Revival home, the only building original to the property, contains dolls, dollhouses, automata, pewter, Staffordshire pottery, and Toby jugs.

Webb didn't hesitate to add new construction to the museum grounds. The Circus Building, completed after her death, was specifically designed to house the remarkable Arnold Circus Parade. Created by Vermont native Roy F. Arnold, the parade captures the excitement of the circus coming to town through 4,000 hand-carved figures that stretch for more than 500 feet. Paralleling the dioramas of the parade are a series of individual carousel figures and vintage circus posters. At the entrance to the Circus Building, one massive diorama contains the sprawling three-ring circus of more than 3,500 tiny figures hand cut and carved by Edgar Decker Kirk, a brakeman for the Pennsylvania Railroad, over a span of more than forty years.

Completed in 1960, the Webb Gallery displays selections from the museum's collection of American paintings. The works trace an artistic trajectory from colonial-era portraiture to early twentieth-century Modernism—with stops in between for Hudson River School landscapes, nineteenth-century folk paintings, luminous seascapes, and vigorous realism from the brushes of such painters as Winslow Homer and Eastman Johnson.

Although the Shelburne Museum is decidedly not a re-created historic village, Webb did have a special affection for structures that embodied the lifestyle of northern Vermont. The thirty-nine buildings set among gardens on the forty-five-acre museum property include a mid-nineteenth-century one-room schoolhouse and a Methodist meetinghouse along with a two-cell jailhouse and the 1890 Shelburne railroad station. Nor did Webb limit herself to the conventions of Vermont village life. She also rescued the 1871 Colchester Reef lighthouse that had guided mariners past dangerous reefs on Lake Champlain.

Visitors are perhaps most surprised by the *Ticonderoga*, a 220-foot Lake Champlain steamboat that rests on the grassy lawn. Webb's husband was less surprised. Years later, Webb reflected that she was nervous about telling him that she had impulsively purchased a steamboat that was about to be scrapped. He was nonplussed, saying, "I don't know; that's not so bad. I think a lot of the other stuff you bought is much worse."

Webb died on November 19, 1960. In her memory, her children constructed the Electra Havemeyer Webb Memorial Building. The exterior shell is modeled on a Greek Revival farmhouse in Orwell, Vermont, that Webb had admired. The interior, however, couldn't be farther in spirit from a farmhouse. It re-creates six rooms of Webb's 1930s Park Avenue apartment, complete with her exceptional collection of Old Master and French Impressionist paintings. In fact, one of the first things

David Lyon

visitors encounter is the Mary Cassatt pastel of a young Electra with her mother. The refined furniture and decorative arts throughout the building are largely as Webb had lived with them in the Manhattan apartment. The building rounds out the picture of Webb's broad taste that could embrace conventional refinement while simultaneously celebrating the straightforward beauty in objects created by untutored hands.

Genteel Rusticity

William Seward Webb and Lila Vanderbilt Webb, Electra Havemeyer Webb's in-laws, created Shelburne Farms between 1886 and 1905. Lila used her Vanderbilt family wealth to bankroll the massive home and model farm on the shores of Lake Champlain. But she didn't stop there. She was also actively involved in designing gardens and furnishing and decorating her family's getaway home.

In 1972, descendants of William and Lila created a nonprofit organization to manage the property. It focuses on sustainable agriculture and makes cheddar cheese from the milk of its own herd of Brown Swiss dairy cows. Visitors are welcome to walk ten miles of trails, view farm animals, and shop in the farm store. The Webb home has been carefully restored and still contains many of the original family furnishings. It operates as a twenty-four-room inn and farm-to-table restaurant, providing an unusual opportunity to experience the Gilded Age lifestyle—if only for a few hours. Shelburne Farms (shelburnefarms.org) became a National Historic Landmark in 2001.

ELKA SCHUMANN'S ACTIVIST FARM
Bread and Puppet Theater, 753 Heights Road, Glover; 802-525-3031; breadandpuppet.org; museum open year-round; free. Check website for summer performance schedule; admission charged.

Elka Schumann traveled around the globe to find her place in Glover, Vermont, as the radical left earth mother of the avant-garde Bread and Puppet Theater. She and her husband, Peter Schumann, nurtured the unruly troupe from its early days of protest performances on the streets of New York to its position as one of the oldest and most influential political theater companies in the country.

Elka Scott was born on August 29, 1935, in Magnitogorsk, Russia, about 1,000 miles east of Moscow. Her mother, Maria Ivanovna Dikareva Scott, was a math teacher. Her father, John Scott, had traveled from the United States, eager to be part of the socialist society taking shape in the recently established Soviet Union. He worked first in a steel mill and later as a journalist for a French magazine. Seeking to establish his own identity, John Scott chose not to use the surname of his father, Scott Nearing, the prominent radical economist, critic of consumerism, pacifist, and advocate for social justice.

David Lyon

Scott Nearing, however, was to have a profound influence on his granddaughter. In addition to providing her an unimpeachable pedigree in progressive politics, he passed along an appreciation for the self-sufficient, back-to-the-land lifestyle that Nearing and his second wife, Helen, neatly encapsulated in their influential 1954 book, *Living the Good Life.* A passionate commitment to social justice and a deep attachment to the land became the threads that ran through Elka's life.

The Scott family left Russia in advance of the German invasion in the buildup to World War II. Following an epic journey by Trans-Siberian Railway and ship, they finally landed in the United States. Elka studied at schools in New York and Berlin, where her family spent four years after World War II while her father was head of the Time-Life News Bureau. Back in the United States, Elka attended high school in Ridgefield, Connecticut, for three years, before graduating from the private Putney School in Putney, Vermont, in 1953. In keeping with its progressive philosophy, the school had hired Scott Nearing as a lecturer.

Elka pursued higher education at Bryn Mawr College, a women's school in Bryn Mawr, Pennsylvania. Disenchanted with what she perceived as her fellow students' preoccupation with their social lives, she elected to spend her junior year in Munich. That's where she met Peter Schumann, a choreographer, artist, and baker, originally from Silesia. The couple married in 1959, a year after Elka graduated from Bryn Mawr with a degree in art history. They settled in the United States in 1961.

Bread and Puppet Theater was founded in 1963 while the Schumanns were living on the Lower East Side of Manhattan. Elka supplied the American activist impulse that drove Bread and Puppet as strongly as her husband's Brechtian Expressionism.

Early performances with fairly modest puppets confronted problems such as rising rents and greedy landlords.

But over time, both the puppets and the company's creative drive to better the world became ever more expansive. Drawing on a background in modern dance and sculpture, Peter Schumann inflated the concept of puppetry to life-size figures wearing papier-mâché masks. The company earned its artistic and political stripes vehemently protesting the Vietnam War, and Bread and Puppet's expressive performance art has taken to the barricades in nearly every social-justice movement since.

In 1974, after several years in residence at ultra-progressive Goddard College in Plainfield, Vermont, the Schumanns found a permanent base on an old dairy farm in Vermont's Northeast Kingdom. It offered enough room for the couple and their five children and for troupe members to create the increasingly ambitious and complex Bread and Puppet productions. Elka took a page from Scott Nearing's book as she raised sheep, made apple cider, tended a big garden, and organized a 2,000-tap maple sugaring operation. Peter baked the dense, nourishing Silesian rye bread that is shared with audience members after every performance.

Elka was quite simply the glue that held the farm and the company together. She kept the books, managed the always precarious finances, and oversaw Bread and Puppet Press. Started in the mid-1980s to create posters, pamphlets, calendars, and other materials to spread the word about the company and its causes, the press has proved to be an important stream of income for company endeavors.

When audience members found their way to the rural farm for a performance, Elka was usually the one to lead them on a tour through the old hay barn turned museum. Filled with giant papier-mâché puppet heads, costumes, props, posters, and signs, it chronicles the company's ongoing artful fight for social justice as well as the evolution of characters in the company's visual lexicon. Elka would pause and talk with affection about the giant puppet heads and the many characters they had assumed over the years. After the tour, audience members would settle onto the bleacher-style risers in the aptly named New Building for the performance and would later spill out into a joyful procession through a hayfield.

Elka's strong artistic instincts made her Peter's most trusted advisor. She was also a performer, often playing the tenor saxophone, flute, or recorder in the company band. Always curious, she became fascinated with Sacred Harp music for its role as an expression of community. She was often credited for much of the musical form's revival in the northeastern United States.

Elka Schumann performed with Bread and Puppet right up until her death on August 1, 2021. She is buried in a pine forest on the remote farm where she helped sustain the vision and energy of what Peter Schumann once described as "a modest little puppet theater—and all we want to do is change the world and save it from going down the drain."

David Lyon

SARAH ORNE JEWETT'S FAMILY HOME
Sarah Orne Jewett House Museum, 5 Portland Street, South Berwick; 207-384-2454; historicnewengland.org; open June through mid-October; admission charged

Sarah Orne Jewett may have hobnobbed with the cream of American and British literary society, but she drew her inspiration from her roots in small-town Maine. That colloquial, even parochial, experience supplied a rich milieu for the sketches, short stories, and novels that made her one of the most widely read and deeply respected regional authors of the second half of the nineteenth century.

Jewett was born on September 3, 1849, in her grandparents' eighteenth-century Georgian home in South Berwick, just thirteen miles up the Piscataqua River from Kittery, Maine, and Portsmouth, New Hampshire. She died in that same home on June 24, 1909. "I was born here and I hope to die here," she once said, as if making a prophecy, "leaving the lilac bushes still green and all the chairs in their places." In the years between, she forged her life as an independent woman and a vigorous prose stylist celebrated as one of America's most prominent literary figures in the decades before World War I.

After growing up in a Greek Revival house next door, Sarah and her older sister Mary inherited their grandparents' home in 1877 and lived there for the rest of their lives. Both properties are now under the stewardship of Historic New England. Jewett's childhood home serves as a reception center, while the house she inhabited as an adult is presented as she lived in it—right down to the thriving lilacs outside the front door.

Built for a sea captain, the two-story house features a gorgeously carved staircase in the front hall. The sisters appreciated such fine architectural details, but didn't hesitate to put their own stamp on the decor. They visited the Centennial Exposition in Philadelphia in 1876, where they discovered and fully embraced the Arts and Crafts style. In contrast to the country mice that readers of her books might have expected, Jewett and her sister were up-to-date sophisticates of their time. They promptly made a strong stylistic statement in the front entry hall, where the stair runner replicates a William Morris pattern and the wallpaper fairly shouts out with a bold tulip figure.

Both Sarah and Mary had attended Berwick Academy, and Sarah read widely from the books in the family library, located to the right of the front door upon entering the house. She also accompanied her father, country doctor Theodore

Jewett, on his house calls to the farming and fishing families living nearby. She later claimed that the intimate experience with vanishing ways of life provided her most valuable education as a writer. Throughout her career, she demonstrated an abiding love of rural Maine life.

Jewett published her first short story in 1868 and her first novel, *Deephaven*, in 1877. The novel's Brandon family home was modeled on her own South Berwick home, sometimes referenced in evocative detail. The dining room at the back of her home contains a massive family heirloom sideboard that inspired the one in

David Lyon

Deephaven. "From the little closets in the sideboard came a most significant odor of cake and wine whenever one opened the doors," Jewett wrote of the piece.

Jewett wrote at a tall Arts and Crafts drop-front secretary desk next to a sunny window on the second-floor landing. She would handle her extensive correspondence in the morning and concentrate on her literary projects in the afternoon, often penning at least 2,000 to 4,000 words a day. She published more than twenty books and innumerable pieces of short fiction, sketches, and children's stories. *The Country of Pointed Firs*, published in 1896, is generally considered her finest work for its loving yet unsparing representation of life in a seaport town well past its heyday, where its often lonely occupants bear up with humor that deflects sorrow. Jewett's friend Henry James (who reportedly made fun of her Maine accent) called the book a "beautiful little quantum of achievement."

By the mid-twentieth century, however, Jewett's work—and, indeed, regionalist writing in general—had fallen out of favor. But the books remained, and a new generation of scholars has rediscovered them, championing Jewett as a chronicler of New England life and a forerunner of modern feminist sensibility. Her tales repeatedly show independent women in hard-won positions of power and influence. In more recent years, her work has been seen in a fresh light as pioneering LGBTQ+ themes.

Jewett herself followed an independent path, choosing to never marry. She always cultivated close female friendships, and for the last three decades of her life, she enjoyed a committed relationship with Annie Adams Fields—possibly the most influential woman in American publishing.

Born into a wealthy family and deeply educated, Annie Adams was twenty years old when she became the second wife of James T. Fields. Her husband was co-owner of America's leading literary publishing house and would soon also assume the editorship of the country's top intellectual and literary journal, the *Atlantic Monthly*. Annie played a central role in selecting authors for both enterprises and presided over the literary salon that the couple held in their home on Charles Street in Boston. She remained a force in American letters until her death in 1915.

Jewett came into the orbit of that salon as an aspiring young writer but soon developed a personal friendship with Annie. When James T. Fields died suddenly in 1881, Annie Adams Fields sought solace in her relationship with Jewett, then thirty-two and becoming ever more famous and successful. In what Henry James coined a "Boston marriage," Jewett and Fields were financially secure and lived together for most of the year. They entertained friends and traveled extensively as a couple. They had numerous nicknames for each other and wrote affectionate letters when they were apart.

Anticipating joining Fields for her birthday in 1883, Jewett wrote, "How I am looking forward to Thursday evening. I don't care whether there is starlight or a fog. ...I am tired of writing things. I want now to paint things, and drive things, and kiss things ..."

David Lyon

The women lived together in Boston during the winter, and Jewett would join Fields at her summer home at Manchester-by-the-Sea on Boston's North Shore. But Fields was less enamored of small-town Maine life and would only occasionally join Jewett when she returned to South Berwick to immerse herself in writing and in the slower pace of life. On the mantel over the fireplace in her second-floor bedroom at the back of the house, Jewett kept a lovely photographic portrait of Fields. Another framed version of the same image appears in the first-floor parlor.

In 1902, a fluke carriage accident left Jewett partially paralyzed and barely able to write. She did, however, act as a mentor to younger writers, most notably Willa Cather, who would become famous as a regionalist author of the Great Plains. The two met in Boston in 1908 and corresponded until Jewett's death the following year. In one letter, Jewett counseled the younger writer that "we must be ourselves, but we must be our best selves."

When Cather's breakthrough novel *O Pioneers!* was published in 1913, she dedicated it to "the memory of Sarah Orne Jewett in whose beautiful and delicate work there is the perfection that endures."

RACHEL CARSON'S EDGE OF THE SEA
Hendricks Head Beach, 22 Salt Pond Road, Southport

Rachel Carson Salt Pond Preserve, 150 ME 32, New Harbor

Ocean Point, East Boothbay

Newagen Seaside Inn, 60 Newagen Colony Road, Southport; 800-654-5242; newagenseasideinn.com; open mid-May to mid-October

Waves crash against behemoth boulders as the tide surges in at the little public beach near Hendricks Head Light in Southport, where the Sheepscot River enters the Gulf of Maine. Tourists aim their phones and cameras to snap the idealized image of the rocky coast of Maine, complete with a squat lighthouse on the point in the background. Those who think of it make videos to capture the sullen roar of the surf.

Marine biologist and writer Rachel Carson had an entirely different vision. As the tide receded, she knelt at the pools the ocean left behind and marveled that

U.S. Fish & Wildlife Service

they teemed with life. At the edge of the sea, she wrote, "the drama of life played its first scene on earth and perhaps even its prelude; where the forces of evolution are at work today, as they have been since the appearance of what we know as life."

In 1953, Carson had recently retired from a fifteen-year career as a writer and editor for the U.S. Fish and Wildlife Service when she had a summer cottage built on Southport Island, west of Boothbay Harbor at the mouth of the Sheepscot River. Born in Springdale, Pennsylvania, on May 27, 1907, she became fascinated by the ocean while studying at the Woods Hole Oceanographic Institute on Cape Cod following graduation from the Pennsylvania College for Women (now Chatham University) in 1929 with a degree in biology. Carson went on to earn a master's degree in zoology from Johns Hopkins University in 1932. Her solid grounding in science was complemented by a reverent sense of wonder and a lyric ability to convey her insights about the natural world. The combination firmly established her as the patron saint of environmentalism.

By the time she built her cottage in Maine, Carson had already published two books that explored the mystery of the sea, establishing her as one of the best-known and most admired nature writers in the country. *Under the Sea Wind*, published in 1941, was followed a decade later by *The Sea Around Us*. Awarded the 1952 National Book Award for nonfiction, *The Sea Around Us* spent eighty-six weeks on the *New York Times* best-seller list and helped make Carson financially secure. Moreover, she received a Guggenheim Fellowship to help pursue her research in the tidal zone that is neither land nor sea. Her cottage, which she called Silverledges, was the perfect place to immerse herself in her subject—and work without interruptions to her already slow pace of writing.

David Lyon

David Lyon

The cottage, now owned by the Rachel Carson Council, is not open to casual visitors. But if her private space for contemplation and composition is not available to Carson fans, many of the spots where she followed the rhythm of the tides and cycles of life are. Her tide pool microcosm is as accessible as ever—maybe even more so thanks to the environmental protections that are her legacy. Hendricks Head was near her summer home, but she also frequented the rim of the salt pond on the shore of Muscongus Bay, not far from Pemaquid Point. The short swath of coast has been set aside by the Nature Conservancy as the Rachel Carson Salt Pond Preserve. Carson often brought Roger Christie, a grandnephew whom she later adopted, with her. It's easy to imagine the young boy's sense of wonder as she pointed out dogwinkles, periwinkles, barnacles, kelp, blue mussels, green crabs, and other creatures that populated the tiny pools of water left by the receding ocean.

A colleague at Fish and Wildlife, artist Robert Hines, often accompanied her to Ocean Point at the southern tip of East Boothbay, a Linekin Bay shore of cracked ledges and ocean cobbles. Many specimens for his illustrations for Carson's 1955 book, *The Edge of the Sea*, were collected here. Although the book delves into the ecology of the Atlantic coast from New England to the mangrove islands of southwestern Florida, much of it was written at Silverledges. Here at her summer retreat, she also grappled with the book that arguably launched the modern environmental movement, transforming the genteel tradition of meditative nature appreciation into an urgent call for environmental action.

Published in 1962, *Silent Spring* warned that "indiscriminate use" of DDT and other pesticides meant to control insects could have devastating effects. With meticulous research and precise analysis, Carson showed the interconnectedness of all forms of life in an ecosystem and demonstrated that introducing toxic agents meant an all-out assault on life itself. It was a radical shift of perspective in an age when regulation of toxic agents fell to agencies whose task was to promote agriculture, not health. Not surprisingly, the chemical industry attacked Carson savagely, labeling her findings "gross distortions." Outraged that she had impugned the motives of big business, Henry Luce's *Time* magazine labeled the book "hysterically overemphatic" and "nonsense."

Writing in *The Guardian* on the fiftieth anniversary of the publication of *Silent Spring*, novelist Margaret Atwood observed, "Many of the personal attacks on Carson were gender specific, shaped by mid-century perceptions about women: their feeble mental capacities, their bleeding-heart sentimentality, their tendency towards 'hysteria.'"

Her critics underestimated the woman they were dealing with. Although she was known for her reserved nature, Carson nonetheless took her case to the public in a CBS television special on April 3, 1963. "We still haven't become mature enough to think of ourselves as only a tiny part of a vast and incredible universe," she told viewers. "Man's attitude toward nature is today critically important simply because we have now acquired a fateful power to alter and destroy nature."

That same year, President John F. Kennedy's Science Advisory Committee recommended more research into the health hazards caused by pesticides. The chairman of the committee, MIT professor Jerome B. Wiesner, was less measured, noting that uncontrolled use of pesticides and other poisonous chemicals could be "potentially a much greater hazard" than nuclear fallout. Stricken with cancer, Carson, alas, did not live to see the passage of the Endangered Species Act in 1966 or the establishment of the Environmental Protection Agency in 1970. But her passionate defense of nature has since passed into the cultural DNA.

When she wasn't exploring the shore, Carson spent time at the Newagen Seaside Inn, originally established in 1816 and rebuilt after a 1943 fire. She often sat on the porch to write or enjoyed lunch and wandered the grounds with Dorothy Freeman, a summer neighbor who became Carson's closest companion. The hotel displays copies of Carson's books and a September 10, 1963, letter she wrote to Freeman expressing her delight at the migrating monarch butterflies they observed at the inn. As usual, she described her careful observations of nature's wonders in precise but evocative prose, noting the "unhurried westward drift of one small winged form after another, each drawn by some invisible force."

After Carson's death on April 14, 1964, Freeman returned to the inn to spread her friend's ashes along the rocky shore, where a plaque reads in part: *Here at last returned to the sea – "to Oceanus, the ocean river, like the ever-flowing stream of time, the beginning and the end."*

LOUISE NEVELSON'S CHILDHOOD TOWN
Farnsworth Art Museum, 16 Museum Street, Rockland;
207-596-6457; farnsworthmuseum.org; open year-round;
admission charged

Louise Nevelson was born on September 23, 1899, in Pereiaslav, Ukraine, and spent her adult life in Manhattan, where she willed herself into becoming one of the leading and most groundbreaking sculptors of the twentieth century. But she grew up in the modest coastal town of Rockland, Maine, where the Farnsworth Art Museum owns one of the world's largest collections of her work.

Five-year-old Leah Berliawsky became known as Louise when she, her mother Minna, and two of her siblings immigrated to the United States in 1905 to escape persecution of the Jewish community. Her father, Isaac, had arrived several years earlier and settled in Rockland, where Louise was educated in the public schools and routinely received her highest grades in art.

In high school, Louise was the captain of the girls' basketball team and was directed into business courses for those destined for office careers. While working in a law office to fulfill her senior-year course requirements, she met wealthy shipping broker and steamship owner Bernard Nevelson, who introduced her to his younger brother Charles. Louise and Charles were married at the Copley Plaza Hotel in Boston in 1920 and began their married life in New York.

Louise never lived in Rockland again. But she hardly turned her back on her family and often returned for visits. It's up for debate whether Maine's fractured rocky shore or her Rockland upbringing had any influence on Louise's artistic vision. But her mother did nurture her daughter's penchant for making a statement through style. Her father worked at a variety of occupations, including shopkeeper, woodcutter, and junk dealer, before gaining financial stability through real estate ventures. As the Berliawsky family's fortunes rose, Minna made sure that she and her daughters were always well dressed. Throughout her adult life, Louise carried her mother's interest in fashion to an extreme, creating flamboyant combinations of ethnic clothing, big jewelry, hats, and scarves. She often accentuated her eyes with mink eyelashes. Her unique flair landed her at least once on an international best-dressed list, but it was her art that ultimately won her lasting acclaim.

Louise and Charles's son, Myron Irving, was born in 1922. He was still a toddler when Louise began taking classes at the Art Students League. The league had been founded in 1875 by artists eager to turn away from tradition and explore new directions in art emanating from Europe. Classes were often taught by American artists who had returned from their own studies in Europe. In addition, the opening of the Museum of Modern Art in 1929 brought the work of many of Europe's most avant-garde artists to the New York public. Louise began her serious study during a time of ferment and excitement about the possibilities of artistic expression.

By the time she traveled to Munich in 1931 to study with painter Hans Hofmann, the Nevelson family business was in serious financial decline and Louise and Charles had separated. Charting an independent course, she soaked up experience throughout the thirties, studying again with Hofmann in New York and also with painter George Grosz and sculptor Chaim Gross. Like many artists struggling to make a living during the Depression, she was employed by the Works Progress Administration. She also assisted Diego Rivera as he painted a series of murals for the New Workers School.

But Nevelson was already gravitating to sculpture. She produced small-scale pieces in terra-cotta, but found her métier in the assemblages of found wooden objects that ultimately propelled her into the top ranks of sculptors both in the United States and abroad. As her monochromatic pieces grew larger and larger, they assumed a monumental majesty. Moreover, they clearly announced that the creation of large-scale sculpture was no longer the exclusive province of men.

Nevelson's career is a study in determination. She was almost sixty years old when a review by Hilton Kramer in the June 1958 issue of *Arts* finally thrust her into the limelight. Writing of her walls of stacked boxes, Kramer proclaimed, "They are appalling and marvelous; utterly shocking in the way they violate our received ideas on the limits of sculpture and on the confusion of genres, yet profoundly exhilarating in the way they open an entire realm of possibility."

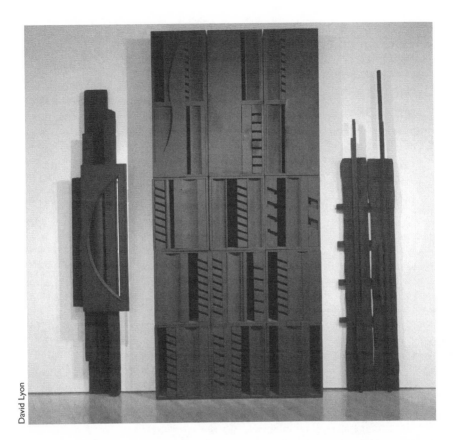

In 1962, Nevelson made her first museum sale, to the Whitney Museum of American Art, which mounted her first major museum retrospective in 1967. Several other museums had featured solo shows of her work before Rockland's rather conservative Farnsworth Art Museum mounted its first Nevelson exhibition in 1979. The *New York Times* described it as a "Down-East Homecoming in Triumph," complete with a presentation of a key to the city, speeches and interviews, and a luncheon with 900 townspeople. Some even presented the artist with scrap wood to incorporate into her work.

In many ways, the exhibition marked a turning point in the museum's embrace of modern art as well as in Louise's relationship with Rockland. Acknowledging that many townspeople had found her to be eccentric, Nevelson told the *Times*, "Of course they laughed here. But I've lived long enough that I have the best laugh."

Nevelson began to donate work to the Farnsworth in the 1980s, including multiple pieces of sculptural jewelry, terra-cotta figures, oil paintings on canvas, collages, and even a portion of her set design for a 1984 production of *Orfeo ed Euridice* at the St. Louis Opera Theatre. Coupled with other purchases and donations of large-scale wooden assemblages, the Farnsworth collection traces Nevelson's artistic development from the 1930s through the 1980s—a remarkable trajectory. The holdings are key for a museum that celebrates Maine's role in American art.

Nevelson's work is in 112 public institutions in the United States as well as in public collections in thirteen other countries. Her awards and honors are too numerous to list. Three years before her death on April 17, 1988, she was honored in the first class of recipients of the National Medal of Arts, receiving the award from President Ronald Reagan. Also in 1985, she received an honorary degree from Harvard University, where she told the assembled crowd that art "gives me my world, it gives me my sanity, it gives me my beauty, and it gives me my life."

An Artful Legacy

Lucy Farnsworth and her family moved into a gracious Victorian home in the 1850s and filled it with all-new furniture. One of six children of William and Mary Farnsworth, Lucy was born in 1838 and lived in the home for the rest of her life. Her father, a successful businessman with interests in everything from real estate to limestone quarries, was also the founder of the Rockland Water Company. His daughter shared his business sense, proving astute at managing his properties and acquiring a sizable stock portfolio.

Upon her death in 1935, Lucy Farnsworth directed that her estate be used to preserve her home and open it to the public and to establish an art museum and art library in memory of her father. Situated on the Farnsworth Art Museum campus and little changed since William's death in 1876, the home remains a time capsule of the merchant family's Victorian taste and lifestyle.

EDNA ST. VINCENT MILLAY'S INSPIRATION

Camden Hills State Park, 280 Belfast Road, Camden; 207-236-3109; maine.gov/dacf/parks; park open year-round, Mount Battie Auto Road open May through October; admission charged

Whitehall, 52 High Street, Camden; 207-236-3391; whitehallmaine. com; open May through October

You don't need to be a poet to be inspired by the sweeping panorama of mountains, islands, and sea visible from the 780-foot summit of Mount Battie, rising a few miles north of Camden. But if you are, you might write the poem that will launch your career.

At least that's what happened to Edna St. Vincent Millay. The event is memorialized by a plaque at the summit: "At the age of eighteen, a frail girl with flaming

David Lyon

David Lyon

red hair left her home in early morning to climb her favorite Camden Hills, where so deeply affected by her surroundings, she wrote 'Renascence.'" The twenty-stanza poem begins with the frequently quoted lines:

> All I could see from where I stood
> Was three long mountains and a wood;
> I turned and looked the other way,
> And saw three islands in a bay.

Neatly summarizing a more complex story, the plaque goes on to note that the "poem received immediate public acclaim and was the inspired beginning of the career of America's finest lyric poet."

Edna St. Vincent Millay was born in nearby Rockland on February 22, 1892. Camden claims her as its own because she grew up in this yachting haven and bustling summer colony with her younger sisters, Norma and Kathleen, and their mother, Cora Buzzell Millay. Although Edna was considered shy, she didn't hide her talents. She won awards from a children's literary magazine, wrote and performed in plays, and edited her high school literary magazine. She graduated in 1909 and, a couple of years later, "Renascence" did help set her on a path to literary acclaim.

Edna entered "Renascence" in a poetry contest and was disappointed when it didn't receive first prize. But it was included in *The Lyric Year* anthology in 1912, which generated some attention for its young author. A personal connection, however, made all the difference. In the summer of 1912, Norma persuaded Edna to recite the poem to guests at Whitehall, a hotel in a former sea captain's house that catered to wealthy summer visitors. Still a lodging, Whitehall recalls the occasion with portraits of Millay and copies of her books in the room where she entranced her listeners.

One audience member, Caroline Dow, head of the YWCA National Training School in New York, had an eye for talent and potential. She arranged for Edna to attend Vassar College, which had been founded in 1861 to provide young women with a liberal arts education equal to that of young men. Edna—or Vincent, as she began calling herself—wasn't necessarily the most dedicated student, but she enjoyed studying languages and the classics and appearing in plays. She graduated in 1917, the same year that *Renascence and Other Poems* was published by Mitchell Kennerley, a publishing house known for championing work that dared to challenge conventional mores.

Edna threw herself heart, soul, and body into the postwar bohemian artistic milieu of Greenwich Village in New York. Her career blossomed in that fertile ground. She published in several important magazines, including *Poetry* and *Vanity Fair*, and also wrote short stories and sketches under the name Nancy Boyd. Both Edna and her sister Norma acted in productions of the Provincetown Players at its Greenwich Village theater. The company had been founded in 1915 to bring innovative works to the stage and helped launch the career of Eugene O'Neill. Edna soon assumed a larger role as a creator as well as interpreter. Her play *The Princess Marries the Page* opened the third season. In 1919, the *New York Times* called her drama *Aria da Capo* "the most beautiful and most interesting play in the English language now to be seen in New York."

Her flair for the dramatic also served her well on the literary reading circuit. Edna was, simply put, a hot ticket. With her red hair, flowing gowns, rich voice, and reputation for flouting social and sexual conventions, she attracted large, adoring crowds wherever she appeared. In the years after World War I, women seeking a freer, more independent lifestyle embraced her for living life on her own terms with neither apology nor regret. Her 1920 poem "First Fig" was their rallying cry:

> My candle burns at both ends;
> It will not last the night;
> But ah, my foes, and oh, my friends –
> It gives a lovely light!

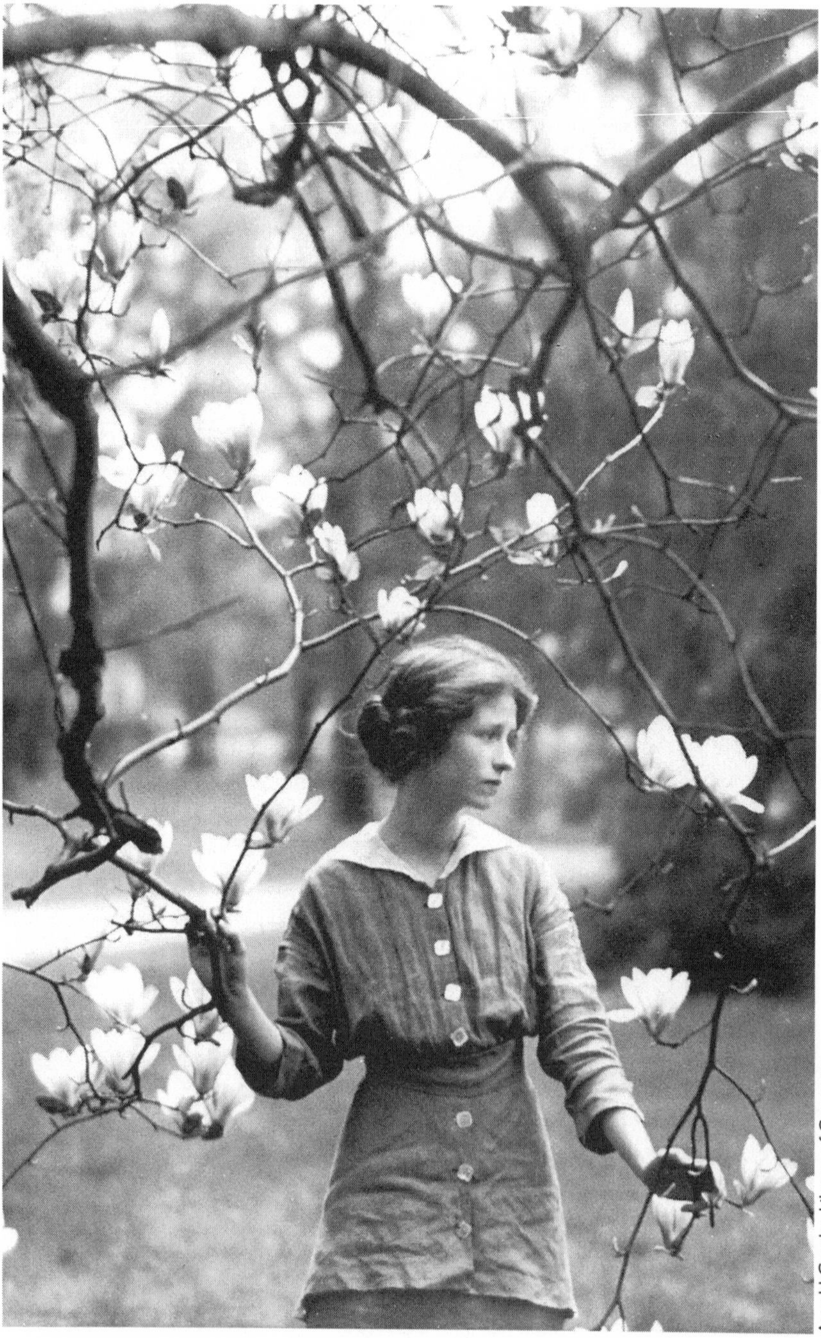

Arnold Genthe, Library of Congress

In 1921, Edna set sail for Europe, where she traveled as a foreign correspondent for *Vanity Fair*. She returned to New York in 1923. It turned out to be a momentous year. She became the first woman to receive the Pulitzer Prize for Poetry for *The Ballad of the Harp Weaver*. Moreover, the liberated woman who had openly pursued love affairs with both men and women—and had broken a few hearts in the process—took a husband. She married Eugen Boissevan, a wealthy Dutch importer who was twelve years her senior. Both of them dabbled in outside affairs, but marriage seemed to suit the couple. Eugen took over managing Edna's career as well as Steepletop, the abandoned farm in Austerlitz, New York, that they purchased in 1925.

Edna craved a quiet place to write, and over the years, they transformed their property into a relaxed country estate with extensive gardens, a tennis court, and guest houses. In addition to writing, she gardened, collected and pressed wildflowers, and kept records of bird sightings. The couple liked to entertain family and friends, who might join them for a nude dip in the swimming pool.

The writer's retreat to the country might seem at odds with the bohemian image that Edna had cultivated during her Greenwich Village years, but it hardly diminished her standing with the public. Appreciative crowds swarmed to hear her when she toured the country to publicize a new book. She made her last national tour in 1939, but continued to use her celebrity to advance causes she believed in. During the early 1940s, she strongly disagreed with America's reluctance to enter World War II. She voiced her concern in the poem "Lines Written in Passion and in Deep Concern for England, France and My Own Country" and in the book *Make Bright the Arrows*. She wrote the radio play *The Murder of Lidice* in 1942 in response to the Nazis' destruction of a Czech village.

Millay often suffered from ill health, relying on morphine to ease her physical pain and allow her to continue writing. Yet Eugen's death in 1949 left her bereft. Edna St. Vincent Millay herself died on October 8, 1950, after a fall down the stairs at Steepletop. The couple's ashes are interred in a birch grove that Millay often visited to enjoy the birdsong.

Her *New York Times* obituary noted that "critics agreed, that Greenwich Village and Vassar, plus a gypsy girlhood on the rocky coast of Maine, produced one of the greatest American poets of her time."

BEATRIX FARRAND'S FINAL GARDEN
Garland Farm, 1029 Bay View Drive, Bar Harbor; 207-288-0237; beatrixfarrandsociety.org/garland-farm; open limited days late June to late September; donation

Landscape gardener Beatrix Farrand spent more than three decades shaping the campus of Princeton University and an equal span creating the gardens at Dumbarton

Oaks in Washington, DC, her most famous project and one that still closely bears her stamp. Yet Farrand is perhaps most widely associated with Mount Desert Island. She formed a lifelong attachment to this second-largest island on the East Coast when her family built a summer home, called Reef Point, in 1883. Many of America's richest families had been drawn to the region's natural beauty celebrated by generations of landscape painters. They built lavish "cottages" that made the town of Bar Harbor a Gilded Age resort rival to Newport, Rhode Island.

Beatrix Cadwalader Jones was born in New York on June 19, 1872, into just such a wealthy, socially prominent family. She was only eight years old when she made her first visit to Bar Harbor. Later, she watched in fascination as her family created a lavish estate and gardens. While still a teenager, Beatrix took over managing the gardens, perhaps unwittingly forging her career path in the emerging field of land-scape architecture.

There were no formal schools in the field, but through a meeting with Mary Allen Robeson, Beatrix arranged a private tutorial in landscape gardening with Mary's hus-band, Charles Sprague Sargent, the first director of the Arnold Arboretum in Boston. The first public arboretum in North America, it was established in 1872 with grounds designed by Frederick Law Olmsted, a pioneer in the profession of landscape design.

Beatrix could not have chosen a richer training ground, where the principle of suiting the plantings to the contours of the land was in full, glorious display. Sargent seems to have been a rather inspired mentor. He encouraged Beatrix to hone her cre-ativity by studying great paintings and by looking closely at nature. He also advised her to visit Europe and absorb the lessons of its many great gardens. It was hardly a tough assignment. Beatrix dutifully complied, broadening her vision through travels in Italy, France, Germany, Holland, England, and Scotland.

By her early twenties, Beatrix was ready to establish her design practice in an office in her mother's Manhattan townhouse. Most public commissions were awarded to men, but Beatrix found plenty of work creating gardens for the fashion-able homes of her wealthy social set. She was the only woman among the founders of the American Society of Landscape Architects in 1899, although she personally preferred the term "landscape gardener."

In 1913, Beatrix married Max Farrand, head of the history department at Yale University and later director of the Henry E. Huntington Library and Art Gallery in San Marino, California. By the time of her marriage, she had been named consulting landscape architect at Princeton and would later work on several other college campuses, including Yale, the University of Chicago, and the California Institute of Technology in Pasadena.

Over the course of her career, Beatrix Farrand completed more than 200 projects, including gardens for the home of J. Pierpont Morgan in New York (now the Morgan Library and Museum), for the White House during Woodrow Wilson's presidency, and for the director's house at the Huntington, where she lived with her husband during his tenure there. During the 1940s, she collaborated on the Landscape Master Plan for the Santa Barbara Botanic Garden. In 1988, the Peggy Rockefeller Rose Garden at the New York Botanical Garden was completed following Beatrix's 1916 design. Of her private garden projects, more than fifty were on Mount Desert Island. Others in New England included Hill-Stead (see page 13) and The Mount (see page 53).

Beatrix and Max continued her practice of spending summers at Reef Point, even as Bar Harbor's cachet began to ebb after World War I. The couple planned to eventually transform the property into a botanical garden and horticultural education center. Max died in 1945, two years before a devastating fire swept through Mount Desert Island, consuming more than 10,000 acres and destroying many of the luxurious cottages and grand hotels.

Beatrix finally realized that she wouldn't be able to make their vision a reality and donated her horticultural library to the Department of Landscape Architecture at the University of California, Berkeley. She dismantled her gardens and had her house torn down. She spent the last four years of her life at Garland Farm, the family farm of her Reef Point property manager Lewis Garland and his wife, Amy Magdalene Garland, Reef Point's horticulturalist.

Architect Robert Patterson incorporated many of the fine architectural elements from Reef Point into the design of an addition between the early nineteenth-century farmhouse and the barn. Although it can't compare to Reef Point, the new home's modest grace was enhanced by the Terrace Garden that Beatrix designed for the rear of the property. She shared the home with her companion and caregiver, Clementine Walter. Each woman's spacious sitting room/bedroom and the shared reception area looked out on the garden, which was meant to delight. Beatrix directed that she would gaze on plants in the pastel shades of blue, pink, and white that she favored. Clementine, on the other hand, would enjoy red and yellow bursts of color. The center portion is devoted to an array of heaths, heathers, and lavenders. The rich carpet of color and aroma serves as an intimate précis of Beatrix's artful garden design, a talent she wielded for so many patrons during her years in Bar Harbor.

David Lyon

David Lyon

Beatrix Farrand died on February 28, 1959, and the property changed hands twice before it was purchased by the Beatrix Farrand Society in 2004. The society has restored the Terrace Garden and nurtures some of the plants that Beatrix transplanted from Reef Point. It has also revived the charming practice of floating a blossom in each of the birdbaths that punctuate the property.

Delights for the Eye Persist Downeast

Garden design aficionados can seek out several surviving examples of Beatrix Farrand's artistry on Mount Desert Island. From 1926 to 1930, she created an impressive garden blending English and Asian styles at The Eyrie, the former summer home of John D. Rockefeller, Jr., in Seal Harbor. Named for his wife, the Abby Aldrich Rockefeller Garden (gardenpreserve.org) is open from mid-July to early September and reaches peak bloom during August. Rockefeller himself is best remembered on Mount Desert Island for the forty-five miles of carriage roads that he had constructed in Acadia National Park (nps.gov/acad). Beatrix advised him on plantings that would accentuate the vistas and bridges along the route, though much of her work did not survive the 1947 fire.

In 1928, Beatrix designed a garden for an estate that was later incorporated into the campus of the College of the Atlantic (www.coa.edu) in Bar Harbor. Located on a slope behind Kaelber Hall, the garden features rough stone walls and staircases that define a series of outdoor rooms. Several of the garden's original rose bushes still survive, while the perennial border features many of the plants that Beatrix often chose for her garden designs.

Acknowledgments

I was thrilled that editor Amy Lyons shared my enthusiasm for this book. I would like to thank her for her feedback and support. Thanks also to the staff at Globe Pequot for their care in shepherding my manuscript into the book that you hold in your hands. I'm very grateful to production editor Jehanne Schweitzer, copy editor Elissa Curcio, book designer Wanda Ditch, cover designer Amanda Wilson, and editorial assistant Greta Schmitz.

Working on this book has reminded me of the great debt I owe to the countless women who have advanced the cause of equal rights. Thanks to each and every one—and to those who continue the struggle for a kinder and more equitable world. I am also indebted to the many individuals and organizations that have preserved the sites that I mention in this book. Without their stewardship these places might not still stand as testaments to women's lives well lived.

Finally, I thank my husband, David Lyon, all the time, but I thought he might like to see it in print. He took many of the photographs that appear in this book. Most importantly, he has believed in me since the day we first met and sometimes helped me to believe in myself.

About the Author

Patricia Harris and her husband, David Lyon, have written more than thirty books on travel, food, and art. Their most recent title for Globe Pequot is *Boston's Historic Hub: A Tour of the Metro Region's Top National Landmarks*. Harris has a personal interest in exploring and celebrating women making their mark on the world. In addition to this title, she is the author of *100 Places in Spain Every Woman Should Go* (Travelers' Tales). She lives in Cambridge, Massachusetts, and can be found online at HungryTravelers.com.